TUNIN' UP

mark Littleton

TUNIN' UP

Daily Jammin' for Tight Relationships

MULTNOMAH

Portland, Oregon

Cover design by Bruce DeRoos
Illustrations by John McPherson

TUNIN' UP
© 1992 by Mark Littleton
Published by Multnomah Press
10209 SE Division Street
Portland, Oregon 97266

Multnomah Press is a ministry of
Multnomah School of the Bible
8435 NE Glisan Street
Portland, Oregon 97220

Printed in the United States of America.

Library of Congress Cataloging-in-Publication Data

Littleton, Mark R., 1950–
     Tunin' up : daily jammin' for tight relationships / Mark Littleton
          p.   cm.
     Summary: Eight weeks of daily devotional readings to help develop "good vibrations" with God, parents, other Christians, boyfriends, and girlfriends.
     ISBN 0-88070-454-3
     1. Teenagers—Prayer–books and devotions.   2. Devotional calendars.   [1. Prayer books and devotions.   2. Christian life.]
I. Title.   II. Title: Tuning Up.
BV4850.L59   1991
242'.63—dc20   91-39829
                                                                      CIP
                                                                       AC

93 94 95 96 97 98 99 00 01 - 10 9 8 7 6 5 4 3 2

To

Nicole and Alisha

great kids
great friends
great joy

CONTENTS

TUNIN' UP

I remember the first time I realized how much relationships mattered. We were in my '64 Ford Mustang whooshing through the falling snow on our way to a ski area to do some quiet schussing and paralleling down the slopes. It was a vintage year Mustang, the first of Lee Iacocca's marvels.

There were four of us in the car. Craig and David were in the back seat, two skiing wizards who also happened to live next door to us at home in Cherry Hill, New Jersey. My younger brother, Steve, sat in the passenger seat, joking. Visibility wasn't bad. But I knew I had to be careful on turns.

Then someone stopped a hundred yards ahead, signaling a turn to the left. I didn't think I needed to brake at that distance.

At fifty yards, the driver still hadn't turned.

My brother murmured, "You'd better slow down." I was doing twenty-five.

At thirty yards, the car was still stuck in the road. It was an old blue Ford Falcon. Craig shouted, "He's not moving!"

I stomped on the brake. Nothing happened. The car kept gliding forward. There was no feel of the bite into the road. I wound the wheel to the right. My heart was pounding like a jackhammer. My mind pitched into slow motion. Then the Mustang smacked the blue Falcon, throwing us all forward. The Falcon bounced away and we skidded right, to a stop. We sat there, stunned.

Tunin' Up

Then I breathed, "Get out." We moved mechanically. Doors clicked open. When I opened the door, a whooshing sound filled my ears. The cold clawed my face. But I felt hot, wet.

An old man unwound out of the blue Falcon. He wore a tattered parka and a grimace. "We're all okay, how 'bout you?" he asked. I nodded. We assessed the damage. His car, nothing. But my Mustang? My dream machine's front left was a mangle of glass, bumper, chrome. The whole left side was bashed in. I wanted to kick something. After exchanging license numbers, we drove to a gas station. I knew I'd have to call my father.

Everyone was dead silent. I couldn't bring myself to get out of the car. What was I going to tell Dad?

At the gas station, the attendant checked the car out. I could drive it, no problem. Then I asked, "How much do you think it'll cost?"

He scratched his head and said, "We ain't no body shop, but I'd call it at three hundred easy."

For the first time I noticed my hands and knees were shaking. What was I going to say to Dad?

I told Steve, Craig, and David I had to call home. When I dialed the number, Dad answered.

"Dad?"

"Mark! Where are you?"

I told him. A sudden sob stabbed into my throat.

"What's wrong?"

I coughed out the words. "Something has happened."

Dad paused. "Is everybody all right?"

"I had an accident. The whole front of the car is bashed in."

Dad asked again, a little louder, "Is everyone all right?"

I glanced at the Mustang sitting forlornly in front of the gas station. "Dad, I'm really sorry. The left headlight is done for. I can drive it, but I bet it's five hundred dollars of damage."

Dad's voice was rising. "Is *everyone* okay?"

I was choking. My throat was taut. "I didn't mean to do it. I was going too fast. I should have slowed down before we got to the point we did. I should have known from how bad the roads were."

Dad, very loud: "Are *you and everyone* all right? No one is hurt, are they?" I paused, astonished. Was everyone okay? It was hard to connect with what he meant. Craig, David, Steve. Of course everyone was okay. But the car? "Yes. Nothing happened to any of us. But the car . . ."

"So everyone's okay?"

"Yes, but . . ."

"Then it's all right. Don't worry about the car. Can you drive it?"

"Yes, I had it checked here at a gas station."

"Okay, get yourself home and we'll see about the car."

I stood there holding the phone. "But it's really messed up, Dad. The whole front . . ."

"Mark! Cars can be fixed. Sometimes people can't. If everyone's okay, everything's okay. All right?"

I nodded and choked.

It was eleven years later that I began to realize what my Dad had really said. The love he communicated in that short conversation continues to speak worlds of truth to me about my father, about life, about Christian faith, and about what's important.

This book is about tuning up your relationships. It doesn't cover everything. Just a few pieces here and there. It would take several if not a whole library of books to satisfy most needs in the relationship area. But this is a start.

We'll look at your relationship with God, your parents, other Christians, boyfriends and girlfriends, and that first date—the interactions that make life a set of musical chairs we constantly fill with new bodies, new outlooks, and new problems.

Every mature person recognizes the need for good relationships as well as the help they can be in our lives. Dwight Eisenhower, president of the United States from 1953 to 1961 and one of the great military leaders of recent history, wrote in his book, *At Ease*, "Always try to associate yourself closely with those who know more than you, who do better than you, who see more clearly than you. Don't be afraid to reach upward. The friendship might pay off at some unforeseen time, but that is only an accidental by-product. The important thing is that such associations will make you a better person."[1]

He was right. It is through our relationships that God transforms us not only to become more like Christ but more ourselves than otherwise possible. Relating leads to refining, which opens the door to real rejoicing.

This book is set up as a devotional[2]—eight weeks of readings with six readings per week. Each reading contains three sections. The beginning section is part of a six-part story that carries through the whole week. As you begin each, remember that what you're reading is part of a story that began on day one and will end on day six.

The second part, subtitled "Perfect Harmony," is a commentary and an insight about what happened that day in the story. It contains a look at Scripture and some spiritual wisdom (hopefully) on the issue.

"Fine Tunin'," the final section, is something for you to do on your own—an application, some questions to answer, a little searching and thinking on your part. I hope you'll take the time to complete it. Any good teacher knows you remember ninety percent of what you do, but less than ten percent of what others tell you. So that's definitely the part you shouldn't skip.

Tunin' Up

Undoubtedly you won't agree with all my thoughts on the way things turn out in these stories. But I hope you'll enjoy them, think about them, and grow deeper in your relationship with God and others as a result. So . . . stay tuned!

Notes
1. Dwight Eisenhower, *At Ease* (London: Hale, 1968).
2. This book is a follow-up to *Beefin' Up: Daily Feed for Amazing Grazing* (Portland, Ore.: Multnomah Press, 1989), Mark's first teen devotional.

WEEK ONE

Detecting a Sour Note

PEOPLE WERE STARTING TO SUSPECT
THAT LISA PANGBORN'S TRYOUT FOR FIRST
CHAIR MAY NOT BE ON THE LEVEL.

MONDAY

Happenin' on a Happenin'

Brandy Wild opened the closet door in the girls' locker room. She hated the jobs Ms. Anson gave her sometimes, but working on the senior play, just being a part of it, made it all worth it. She hit the light and after she stepped in, the creaky door slowly closed behind her. She bent to get the cleanser and brushes that had to be used on the stage props to get them to glisten. She was confident their student production of *Cats* would be excellent.

She was about to open the door, when she heard whispering voices.

"It's locker 413," one voice said. Whoever it was, they obviously believed that no one would know they were there.

"You've got the pack."

"Definitely. Marlboro's. Her brand."

Brandy stiffened and waited. A locker squeaked open. Her heart banged into full throttle. What was going on? She nudged the light switch down, then peered out through the slit in the partially open door. Claire Reims and Hannah Lipscomb stood at one of the lockers opening a purse.

"This'll put her out of the lead for good," Claire said.

Brandy watched with fear and fascination as the two girls crunched a red and white pack of cigarettes into the purse. Claire had been bumped from the number one solo part in *Cats* of Grizabela, the character who sang the hit song, "Memory," in favor a rival named Janice Larkin. Janice had her problems, including smoking, which was the bane of the director's existence. Ms. Anson warned repeatedly that any singers in major roles caught smoking would be removed from their part. But Janice had quit smoking the previous summer specifically so she could play Grizabela. Ms. Anson notified everyone of the selections the week before. Plenty of pushing and tugging continued as different students vied to grab better positions. Claire and Janice had been rivals for years, from choir and chorus to all the plays.

Brandy trembled in the darkness of the closet, wondering if she should step out and scare them away. But what if the two girls confronted her? And how could she be sure of what they were doing?

She decided to sit tight, make no noise, and wait.

Moments later, Claire closed the locker and she and Hannah hurried out. Brandy breathed more deeply now. When she was sure they weren't coming back, she hurried out of the closet, forgetting about the cleanser and brushes. Halfway down the hall to the stage she remembered and had to run back.

When she reached the stage area, though, everyone had gathered to hear a brief speech. Ms. Anson began, "There are rumors that some of you girls have been smoking. We're all going to the locker room now and have an inspection."

She turned to Mr. James, her assistant director, and asked him to keep the boys working on the music. Then she led the girls toward the locker room.

Perfect Harmony

I once said to a friend, "You know, I don't think I ever see you sin."

He laughed and answered, "Would you like to know some of my sins?"

I thought about it. "No, actually I don't. Because then I'd have to confront you about it and I hate confrontations."

Many of us are like that. We'll avoid a confrontation with someone about a misdemeanor or minor crime without a blink. We'd rather ignore the sin, forget that it ever happened, and hope it "just goes away."

It rarely does. Unfortunately, all of us are at times witnesses of foul deeds, like Brandy. How do you feel about such wrong doings? What do you think you'd do? How easy is it for you to corner a friend and "tell him his wrong?" Some people take great pleasure in pointing out one's foibles and failures. But most of us don't enjoy such words, at least face to face. We'll bash someone around behind her back, but going head to head with a friend, neighbor, or acquaintance about genuine sin can be a hair-raising experience.

Still, it's important for Christians to learn to "speak the truth in love," to "tell a person his fault," to "restore" someone who has sinned. Paul wrote to the Galatians, "Brothers, if someone is caught in a sin, you who are spiritual should restore him gently. But watch yourself, or you also may be tempted" (Galatians 6:1). Paul speaks specifically of believers, but certainly the principle holds in all relationships. Jesus tells us in Matthew 18:15, "If your brother sins against you, go and show him his fault, just between the two of you." Jesus was not singling out believers or unbelievers. He meant anyone who sins. In fact, speaking to them of their fault may well be the means by which they come to Christ. Parents are to discipline their children whether they've come to faith or not. The Scriptures say we're responsible for all our conduct regardless of our personal beliefs. The Ten Commandments apply to all of us even if we're not Christian or Jewish.

On the other hand, we must also be clear that our

friend has truly sinned. It can't be a gray issue, or something that's a matter of opinion. There's a story about a golfer who, on the first tee, was standing well forward of the marker to take his shot. One of the club members saw him and said, "Sir, you must be a new member here. You should know you can't take your first shot eight feet ahead of the marker."

The man ignored his critic and continued to set up his shot. "Sir," argued the second man. "I must remind you to go back to the marker." The golfer said nothing and only worked on his follow through.

"Sir," said the exasperated critic. "I am chairman of the greens and I will have to report you to the board."

The golfer spun around and replied evenly, "In the first place, sir, I am not a new member. In the second place, I have been a member of this club for nearly a year and you are the first person who has spoken to me." He paused and swung his club again. "And in the third place, this is my second shot."

Make sure you know whereof you speak before-speaking.

Fine Tunin'

1. How do you handle confrontational situations? Freeze up? Hyperventilate? Are you afraid of rejection? Those are natural responses. Take a look at how Paul handled such a confrontation in Galatians 2:11-21. _____

2. What would you do in Brandy's situation? Outline a few possible strategies and plans of action. _____

TUESDAY

A Ticklish Spot

Janice was obviously surprised and unprepared for what happened. Two other girls were caught with cigarettes, but they were in lesser roles. Ms. Anson was furious with Janice. The pretty, blond girl denied the cigarettes were hers and tried to explain she'd been set up. But Ms. Anson didn't believe her. Janice had been known as a smoker for years, and though it wasn't against school rules, Ms. Anson was adamant.

"I can't keep you in your role, Janice," she fumed. "I'm let down and hurt."

Janice stood before the group in tears. "I swear, Ms. Anson, I don't know anything about this."

"You're saying you've been set up?"

Janice shook her head. "I don't know. I don't smoke anymore. I've wanted to play this role ever since last year, when you announced the senior play would be *Cats*. I don't know how they got there."

Ms. Anson surveyed the group. She was a plump, gray-haired woman, skilled in play direction. She had dictated Jefferson High's plays for decades. She was also a stickler for rules. "Anyone know anything about this?"

Immediately, Brandy's heart jumped. No one looked her way. She was just one of the stage crew. She'd also had her own run-ins with Claire and Hannah. They were part of the "in" group—pretty, aggressive, and competitive. They had ways of nailing someone who talked.

Ms. Anson's voice rang out again. "I repeat: Does anyone know how these cigarettes got into Janice's purse?"

Janice glanced hopefully around at the group. No one answered. Brandy noticed Claire and Hannah appeared perplexed and innocent.

"Janice, I'm sorry. You'll have to step down."

Janice burst into tears again, but Ms. Anson was not easily swayed. She said again, "This is a very bad thing to happen at the beginning of our play, girls. Any more of this, and the culprit is out of the play completely. Rules are for keeping, not for breaking."

Brandy's mind was numb with fear. Should she speak up? She raised her hand. "Ms. Anson?"

The director turned toward Brandy. "Yes?"

All the girls swung around to look into her eyes. Brandy froze. She felt as though she couldn't breathe. Ms. Anson said, "Do you know anything about this?"

Brandy caught a hard gaze from both Hannah and Claire and several others. She searched for something to say, then blurted, "I just wondered if you want me to get back to cleaning the props?"

Girls rolled their eyes. Several snickered.

"Leave it to Wild to get us all going," someone joked.

Ms. Anson shook her head. "This isn't a joke, girls. Get back to work and no more of this nonsense. Claire, I'd like to talk to you."

Brandy watched with despair as Claire bounced up to Ms. Anson like a happy puppy. *She'll get exactly what she wanted now*, Brandy thought miserably.

Perfect Harmony

Injustice is common in our world. People are done dirty, done wrong, done bad, and done in. Frequently, the bystanders say nothing. They "don't want to get involved." They'd rather not "step forward and be counted" lest the accused turn on them.

Yet, Christians must act. We cannot step aside and pretend we don't care. We can't remain silent.

One of the worst cases of injustice ever recorded concerns Ota Benga, a twenty-three-year-old Congolese pygmy. An African explorer named Samuel Verner brought him to the United States to appear in the 1904 St. Louis Exposition. Afterwards, a tribal war prevented Verner from taking Mr. Benga back to the Congo. He turned the four-foot-eleven pygmy over to the director of the Bronx Zoo, William Hornaday. The director gave Mr. Benga a spot in a cage with an orangutan named Dohong and a parrot.

Immediate protest arose from both the black community and the clergy who perceived this as an attempt to foster a belief in evolution. A committee of clergymen appealed to the mayor with no result. Hornaday claimed Mr. Benga was happy and free to go wherever he wanted. Mr. Benga himself spoke no English and could not answer for himself. Nonetheless, he later was released even though he continued to attract great crowds as he promenaded around the grounds in a sporty white suit. He slept at night in the monkey house. However, the crowds annoyed Benga and he once had to fight them off with his bow and arrow. In the end he left the zoo and was taken care of by institutions and individuals. He remained unhappy but had no funds to return home. No one came forward to help him return home. He shot himself in 1916.[1]

In Benga's case some Christians began to correct an injustice. But they stopped too soon. They should have returned him to his homeland.

The point, though, is the same. We as Christians cannot ignore the victimized, hurting, homeless, and persecuted. Brandy Wild could no more forget what she saw in the locker room than visitors to the Bronx Zoo could catcall at Ota Benga and pretend he was an ape. We must act. We must correct the wrong, if we can. And at all costs, we must confront the wrongdoer. Not only their lives, but our souls depend on it.

Fine Tunin'

1. Read the passage about the crowd during Jesus' trial before Pilate in John 19:1-16. How easy might it have been in that context to defend Jesus? Why do you think none of the disciples came to his help? _____

_____

_____

2. In a sense, Brandy already failed by not speaking up. But how easy would it have been for you? What thoughts race through one's mind in such a situation? What can a Christian do in such a place to help herself stand firm? _____

_____

_____

WEDNESDAY

No Sleep Tonight

Brandy couldn't sleep that night. She got up three times, tried to eat some chocolate cake, even read from her Bible. She believed the Bible could help her solve problems, but her knowledge of the Scriptures was limited. The only thing she knew was that she couldn't let it sit.

The next day at school, Janice didn't appear in English class, the one class Brandy had with her. Ms. Anson put Claire in Janice's role, and Claire talked her into giving Hannah a leadership position in the chorus. Brandy battled a case of nerves and anger as well as an incriminating and grating sense of guilt. That afternoon, she called Clark Benson, a young married man who worked with the youth at church. He was surprised at hearing her voice. "Calling from school, huh? Must be something like a math test." He loved teasing the girls, particularly Brandy.

"It's serious, Clark."

His voice immediately softened. "Go ahead."

"I don't want to tell you the exact situation, just this: if you saw someone do something hurtful to another person without that other person knowing who did it, what would you do?"

Clark paused, then said, "I'd confront the person who did it, in private. If they wouldn't listen to me, then I'd go with a second party, probably someone whom you know would command some respect from the guilty party. Actually, it's all spelled out in Matthew 18, about the middle. Read that, and I think you'll understand."

"But I don't think the people involved are Christians."

25

Clark paused and Brandy waited for some other answer. The word *confront* terrified her. Who was she to confront someone like Claire Reims?

Clark went on, "I really don't think it matters. The principle is the same. I think it's all part of being a peacemaker."

Brandy swallowed. "You really know how to make it easy, don't you?"

"I'll be glad to help you anyway I can, Bran, but ultimately that's what it means to be a Christian. Sometimes you have to be like a turtle."

"What's that?" Clark was always using these pet maxims.

"The turtle makes progress only when he sticks his neck out."

Brandy grimaced. "Thanks a lot."

Perfect Harmony

What a tough situation! Who would want it? And waiting only made it worse. The passage of time always makes it more difficult to take the steps we should take. In the time we procrastinate the devil can fill our heads with all sorts of horrid images that make us shy away from the real responsibility.

Somehow Brandy needed to speak with Claire and Hannah—alone. That was the hard part. In a group or with several others present, it would be easier. But the first step should always be personal and private. We should not talk to anyone else about it. No gossip. No rumors.

What we fear is anger, rejection, even violence. Who knows what Claire and Hannah might do to Brandy? In their high school they obviously had some power because of their activities and looks. Other kids revered them, looked up to them. Brandy was just another one of the crowd. A nobody. Who was she to accuse them?

Frankly, who she is doesn't matter. An honest witness on the stand has the same power as the president of the United States. Our testimony has as much weight as anyone else's, if we are an eyewitness.

Still, as Brandy contemplates what she was about to do, she should think of several things. Let me outline it in the word *confront*.

Caution. Don't leap into the fray; walk in quietly and ask for a hearing.

Obligation. You have an obligation about this to Jesus, the victim, your friends, yourself, and even the one who has sinned. Restoring them can change their life.

Nervousness. You will be nervous, so expect it and don't worry about it.

Forthrightness. Don't go to accuse, but to speak directly and kindly.

Realism. Remember, people are sinners. Be realistic. Don't expect an amazing turnaround; perhaps the best you can get is a fair hearing.

Openness. Go with a willingness to listen as well as to help.

New Life. Your goal is to breathe life into the one who has sinned, to restore them, not to knock them down.

Trust. Trust that God will work in the midst of the situation.

James Dobson once wrote, "The right to criticize must be earned, even if the advice is constructive in nature. Before you are entitled to tinker with another person's self-esteem, you are obligated first to demonstrate your respect for him as a person. When a relationship of confidence has been carefully constructed, you will have earned the right to discuss a potentially threatening topic. Your motives will have been thereby clarified."[2]

While Brandy couldn't easily win Claire and Hannah's respect in the time she had, she could do it in the context of the confrontation. It's difficult, but not impossible.

Fine Tunin'
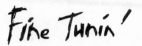

1. Read how Nathan confronted David about his sin in 2 Samuel 12:1-14. Why do you think Nathan took the creative approach? How did that help? _____

_____

_____

2. How could Brandy apply the truths of 2 Samuel 12:1-14 to her situation? What creative steps might she bring to her circumstance? _____

_____

_____

THURSDAY

Blank Black Terror

Brandy deliberated about saying anything to Claire the following Monday. Janice had been out for three days. Brandy knew it was unfair.

She tried to think of some way of approaching Claire and Hannah—like happening upon them in a bathroom or catching them alone at practice. But every time she passed or saw them, she tightened up and couldn't muster the courage.

She called Clark again and gave him a bit more detail without providing names. He encouraged her, told her that fear was natural, and to remember that God was with her. But she knew she'd feel braver if someone went with her. But Clark didn't volunteer. He kept saying that it had to be in private, and she should do it alone.

On Tuesday afternoon with Janice still absent from school, Brandy steeled herself for the moment. She walked over to the group as casually as she could. When there was a lull in the talk, she said hoarsely, "Claire, can I talk to you and Hannah for a moment?"

Claire gave her a quick once over and said cattily, "Who are you?"

Brandy's heart pounded right into her throat, but she didn't back down. "I'd just like to talk to you privately for a moment."

Claire shrugged. "You can say anything to me and my friends."

Brandy chewed her lip. "It's about Janice Larkin."

Claire's face blanched only slightly. "Okay. You want Hannah to come, too?"

"Yes."

Claire motioned to Hannah. "Let's make this quick. I have to do my song."

Perfect Harmony

Confrontations can be absolutely terrifying. We'll do anything to melt onto the pavement and disappear through a crack.

But it never happens. Reality is never easy.

Yet, what are they going to do? Hire a hit man? Scratch your eyeballs out? Be realistic! Laugh a little. The worst they'll do is yell, maybe even get nasty. Unless you're dealing with the Mafia or a cocaine ring, you're in little danger.

But that doesn't make it any easier.

Even John Wayne didn't like being confronted. For all his size, he happened to have small feet. On an elevator one day a woman glanced at his feet and commented, "My, your feet are small!" The Duke, huge and imposing, remained silent until he reached his floor. Then on his way out of the elevator he retorted, "They're size ten and a half." He started down the corridor, then whipped around to leave her with a final shot: "E's!"

Notice: He didn't chew that poor lady up and spit her out. And that was John Wayne! Oh, you don't know about him? Cowboy actor? Green Beret actor? Big? Strong? Mean? He was tough.

Just the same, you should be prepared for a strong reaction. You never know how a person will respond to a solid shot to the self-esteem. Especially if they've really done something wrong. The Scripture says, "Do not let any unwholesome talk come out of your mouths, but only what is helpful for building others up according to their needs, that it may benefit those who listen" (Ephesians 4:29).

A good word can calm, restore, enliven, rebuild. Keep plenty of them in your pocket for ready distribution.

Fine Tunin'

1. Read Galatians 5:22-23, the passage on the fruit of the Spirit. How would these qualities help Brandy in her situation? _____

_____

_____

2. What characteristics do you think are most important in a confrontation situation? What ones would you pray for and work on? _____

_____

_____

FRIDAY

The Danger Zone

As they clopped off stage, Brandy realized she hadn't planned where they would talk. She found an empty classroom near the auditorium. No one said anything until they stood inside, with Claire lolling in the doorway, as if planning to make a fast exit. Brandy said, "I think we should shut the door."

Claire's eyes slit, but she quietly closed it. "All right Wild, what's this about?"

Brandy breathed deeply to keep herself from hyperventilating. "I was in the locker room the other day when you put the cigarettes in Janice's purse."

Hannah swore, but Claire stepped forward menacingly. "Oh, and I suppose you're going to expect a bribe or something?"

Brandy didn't move, even though Claire stood only a few feet from her face. "No, I don't want a bribe. I want you to tell Ms. Anson the truth."

Hannah laughed. Claire said, "Do you know what we can do to you?"

Brandy nodded. "I suppose, but I'm a Christian and . . ."

"Oh, so this is all religious stuff, is it?"

Brandy held her ground. "Look, I don't care what you do. God'll take care of me. But right is right, and what you did was wrong. I want you to go with me to Ms. Anson and tell her the whole story. I'm sure she'll understand . . ."

"Oh, right! Like the way she kicked Janice out. Forget it."

Brandy stilled her shaking by leaning on a desk. "Then you refuse?"

"Absolutely."

"All right, then I'll have to go to the second step."

Claire turned to Hannah. "This girl's looking for a beating, you know?"

Hannah nodded. But neither girl moved forward. Though Brandy was timid, she did play softball. She knew she could put up a good fight if she had to.

Claire said, "What do you mean?"

Brandy took another deep breath. "I'll get two impartial witnesses, all five of us will meet, and we'll discuss the situation."

"And who will the witnesses be?"

"The principal, Mr. Evans, and Mr. James, the assistant director."

Claire's jaw was tight and her face livid. "Are you threatening me?"

Brandy shook her head. "No, I'm just telling you what I will do if you don't go with me now to talk to Ms. Anson."

Claire looked helplessly at Hannah. Brandy stood silent. Then Claire said, "It's two against one here."

"I know."

Claire cursed. "Why are you doing this?"

"Because you were unfair to Janice."

Claire cursed again. "All right. Go outside. Give Hannah and me a minute."

Perfect Harmony

Hurray, Brandy. What a show! Superb! I mean, this girl has guts.

And that's precisely what it will take. No one likes a confrontation, but above all we need simple courage, guts! We see that quality portrayed all over the silver screen.

33

They all have it. But they're fictional characters. Fiction is easy. Anything can happen.

Reality . . . does it ever go like that? Sure. Did you ever think that Claire and Hannah might be as afraid of Brandy as Brandy was of them? None of us know what really goes on in the heart of a person. And many of us are terrified little twits half-scared of our own shadows until we've tried acting courageously a few times. Then it gets easier.

But that first time is murder.

Just like a first date, a first body block, a first time at bat, a first speech. They all terrify. But once the stage fright is over and we're on, it turns out not to be so bad.

And remember a word from God: "Do not fear, for I am with you; do not be dismayed, for I am your God. I will strengthen you and help you; I will uphold you with my righteous right hand"(Isaiah 41:10).

Fine Tunin'

1. What do you do about fear? Read Philippians 4:6-7 and 2 Timothy 1:7. How do these truths help? _____

_____

_____

2. Write a prescription for courage. How does it happen? What enables us to act courageously in the midst of harrowing circumstances? _____

_____

_____

WEEKEND

Captain Courage

Brandy stood outside the door, while Claire and Hannah shouted inside. A few minutes later, they both came out, looking shaken and weak. "Okay, we'll talk to Ms. Anson."

As they walked to see the hard-line musical director, Claire suddenly said, "What's to prevent us from accusing you of doing it?"

Brandy stopped. Strangely, she knew what to say. "Nothing's to prevent you, except Ms. Anson will probably see I have no motive to set up Janice, and you have complete motivation. I don't think she's that dumb."

♪

Things didn't turn out precisely as Brandy had hoped. Ms. Anson was angry and decided to spend several days thinking about what to do. She told Janice she could have the part back and made Claire and Hannah tell the whole crew what they had done. They felt humiliated and angry, but they came clean. Everyone talked about what kind of punishment should be given and Janice herself asked that Claire be given her original position. Ms. Anson nixed that and ended up putting both girls back in the chorus. In the end, they both decided to drop out of the play altogether.

The school steamed with rumors and a number of kids hit Brandy with rejection and anger, calling her a rat and that she shouldn't have made the girls confess. However, a number of others, including Janice, asked her to join their group and soon she made some fast friendships.

It turned out to be a rough year. But on the Saturday before the last day of school, Janice, Brandy, and several others went to the mall together. They happened to pass a Christian bookstore and when Janice decided she wanted to go in, she happened to find a wooden plaque with the word *Courage* on it and a slogan: "The decision to do what's right even though all the world might stand against you."

She bought it later and presented it to Brandy at graduation, saying, "I admire you both as a person and for what you did. I love you." Both girls promised to write and keep in touch. Brandy felt sure it was the beginning of a lifelong friendship.

Perfect Harmony

Everyone likes a happy ending. And there is one here, in a sense. But it wasn't an easy ending. Because of sin, relationships were hurt and broken. Certainly forgiveness was possible. Certainly Claire and Hannah could have recovered from their mistake.

But it is not always to be. Unless a sinner finds freedom in repentance and forgiveness, sin feels like a weight that everyone sees whenever that person steps into the light. That's part of the danger of confrontation. Will the sinner truly repent? Only God knows the answer to that one. We must obey, regardless.

Martin Niemoeller, a pastor during the years of Adolph Hitler's reign over Nazi Germany, wrote: "When they came for the Communists, I didn't speak up, because I wasn't a Communist. When they came for the Social Democrats, I didn't speak up because I wasn't a Social Democrat. When they came for the Jews, I didn't speak up because I was already in a concentration camp. By then nobody was left who could or wanted to protest."

When Christians remain silent, the world spins out of control.

By way of contrast, if you ever have a chance to look at the Declaration of Independence in the Archives Building in Washington, D.C., you'll certainly notice the famous signature of John Hancock, bold and swirly in the middle. Another signature, though, might escape your notice. It's "Charles Carroll of Carrollton." Interesting that he signed both his name and his town. Why? It's said that as Carroll signed his name, someone noted that there were many men by that name. He would be a hard man to find if the British came for revenge. Carroll was a rich man and had much to lose if the Americans lost the Revolution. But as his friend spoke, Carroll leaned down and added the words *of Carrollton*. He wanted no one to mistake who he was. He threw his lot in with those other signers with zeal and courage.

In a sense that is what each of must do as believers. We've thrown our lot in with the truth, with morality, with Christ, with goodness, righteousness, and love. We must stand for it whenever and wherever we can.

Fine Tunin'

1. Do you want courage? Read Matthew 10:16-31. What truth is Jesus teaching in this passage? How can they help you in the daily circumstances of life? _____
_____
_____

2. What problem, sin, or evil do you know about that you should speak against? What can you do to get involved today? _____
_____
_____

Weekend

Notes

1. Amy Wallace, Erving Wallace, and David Wallechinsky, "Man in the Zoo," *Parade Magazine*, 3 January 1982, 28.

2. James Dobson, *What Wives Wish Their Husbands Knew About Women* (Wheaton, Ill.: Tyndale House, 1978).

WEEK TWO

Squeaking Out That First Serenade

HOPING TO SET JUST THE RIGHT MOOD ON HIS FIRST DATE WITH SELMA, LOWELL HIRED A BAND TO SERENADE THEM THE ENTIRE EVENING.

MONDAY

Hooked

Drew Hostetter took his usual seat at the lunch table. About ten other friends ate at the same table and the chatter was fairly usual—sports, rock groups, an upcoming football game.

He opened the bag lunch his mom made him, looked up, and briefly surveyed the huge cafeteria. A moment later he noticed her. She'd been sitting at the next table with a group of girls for several weeks now. He knew her name—Michelle Pellegrino—but not much more. Her sleek black hair, olive skin, and dark eyes instantly attracted him. He'd caught her eyeing him several times. Every time their eyes almost met, his heart beat wildly in his chest. He knew she was a sophomore like him, and had a boyfriend. But a classmate commented that she'd broken up twice in the last year.

Drew had gone out on a few dates prior to his sophomore year. But no one steady. With a special Christmas dance coming up, he'd thought a lot about taking someone. But was she interested? Something about the way she flinched away every time he looked up made him think she might be.

♪

Michelle talked gaily among her friends at the lunch table. She'd gotten in with this group because of a social club that one of the girls from chorus started. She tried hard not to gaze at the boys gathered at the next table. But Drew's light complexion and wavy blond hair turned her on immediately. Her Italian mother always said opposites attract. She noticed his face reddened several times when she looked up and caught him staring at her. A blush? She wasn't sure. He always turned away and began talking briskly to whoever was next to him.

Sometimes it infuriated her, the way boys took so long to make a move. She asked several friends about him, but none knew him well. Just that he was a good student, played baseball, and was a sophomore.

She had already decided that if her on-again off-again boyfriend, Dave Barrack, asked her to the Christmas dance she'd go only if no one else asked. She hoped Drew might get interested. But he seemed shy. He'd never said a word to her.

The one hope she had was an upcoming English field trip to see a play, Shakespeare's *Merchant of Venice*. It was being performed by a local theater group. All the sophomore classes were supposed to go. She thought she might be able to engineer a seat on the same bus, if only Dave didn't interfere.

Perfect Harmony

Figuring out a way to make that first contact with a girl or a guy can be one of life's most troublesome questions. Especially if you're not used to it. Especially if it's the first time. Asking a girl out for a first date probably shakes up more guys on a weekday night than the worst bio tests. Why is taking the plunge so difficult?

There are many reasons. Lack of experience. Shyness. Fear of rejection.

That's the big one. What if I call her up and she laughs? "Drew Hostetter! You've got to be kidding!" Or what if she doesn't even know who I am? "I'm in English.

You know the seat in the back by the window." "Oh, yeah, you're the one with the funny nose and the weird hair. Well, I'm busy anyway." There's only one thing worse than having some woman turn you down, and that's your friends knowing she turned you down.

And what about the ladies? What happens when you're hopelessly in love with some guy in U.S. History and you're getting calls from everyone but him? Or from no one? Or consider when the one you love does call and you have to answer, "I'm sorry, my mom doesn't let me date yet." At any rate, introductions rarely go as planned. Few of us pull off a smooth invitation on that first time around. In fact, that may be part of the fun. Stammering, worrying, your heart in your mouth, your lips dry, your knees quivering, and your little brother saying, "Oh, I've seen her around. What a dogface!"

But don't fret. It'll be over in a flash, the date will be made and then all you'll have to do is figure out where to put your hands. Still, ideas come with time, so even that one isn't real difficult. A truth to remember is this: the only way to get experience is to make a mistake and try again. As the old Chinese proverb goes, "Every journey begins with the first step."

Fine Tunin'

1. Making a first date, breaking that iceberg, is no easy matter. Look at the exchange in Solomon's Song in chapter 1. What do you see in this passage about the lovers' fears and anxieties? How do they quell them?

2. If you've never had or made a date, what steps might you take to make it happen? Whom could you go to for advice? Why not seek them out and ask a few planned questions about your worries?

TUESDAY

Planned Encounter

A week later, Michelle and a friend named Cheryl Hanes spotted Drew and several of his friends boarding the bus to the play, including a guy Cheryl knew named Curt Hosson. Cheryl had known Curt since fifth grade, even though they weren't friends and had never dated. The plan was for her casually to get him to come over with Drew and make some introductions. It was a bit sticky, working out the logistics. But they figured if Romeo and Juliet could pull it off, so could they.

Just as they were about to climb on the bus, one of the teachers said to the lineup, "It's filled. You'll have to take another bus."

There were several groans, but Michelle took Cheryl's elbow. "Wait a minute. There might be something."

Sure enough, as the crowd disappeared, the teacher called to the girls, "There are two more seats. Want them?"

Cheryl giggled and they both clambered up the bus stairs. Drew sat in the back, horsing around with his friends. The two vacancies were up front.

Drew noticed Michelle in the crowd immediately. He recognized Cheryl Hanes, though he didn't know her either. He didn't have a chance or the courage just to walk up to them. The whole back of the bus began singing a rendition of a Bryan Adams tune, but he vigilantly kept his eyes on the two girls outside. When they finally took the seats in the front, he tried to think of a way to get up there.

He turned to Curt. "You know Michelle Pellegrino?"

"Cute chick. Yeah."

44

"She's in the front seat with Cheryl Hanes."

Curt said, "Yeah, I know Cheryl."

"All right, we have to come up with a plan. Maybe we can sit with them."

"I don't know. I could go for Michelle more than Cheryl."

"Forget it, Hosson, she's mine."

Curt grinned. "All right, let's see what we can do."

The bus ground into motion. Groups formed, there was plenty of singing and joking going on. But when some began walking up and down the aisles, the teacher yelled that everyone had to stay in their seats.

Perfect Harmony

Where there's a will, there's a way. When two guys get together on strategy, anything can happen. People meet and pair off in a multitude of ways. For every couple there's a story. And for every story, a few fairy tales.

Dating is important. While Paul did advise some of his disciples that they should think about the possibility of singleness, most of us will eventually date, court, and marry. For some, it's love at first sight. For others, it's love after you've kissed a prince. Still others have to kiss a lot of frogs before they even get close to Mr. Right.

Just the same, dating doesn't have to be as scary as it feels. Youth groups can help a lot simply by sponsoring parties, fellowships, and get togethers where guys and girls can socialize and develop a few conversational skills. Here are a few tips to make that first or dream date happen:

1. Take advantage of social events at your church. However large your church, each one offers its unique contribution. Even if your group is small, it has

advantages. God has put you where you are for a purpose.

2. Don't worry about falling in love. Simply get to know as many people as possible. Sometimes the physical and emotional chemistry is there. But if it's not, don't worry. Love is not a feeling, but an action, a choosing. One can just as much choose to love someone as fall in love. In fact, the former is more realistic and better. Falling in love is something that just happens. Making a conscious choice is taking control of your own destiny.

3. Spend time with groups before pairing off. Many young people are so eager to get a girlfriend or boyfriend it becomes their only waking desire. But there is much to be said for just hanging around with the group. You don't have to be a wit, carry the conversation, and "stand out." You can learn by watching others.

Fine Tunin'

1. Read how God brought Isaac and Rebekah together in Genesis 24:1-67. Granted, this was another culture and outlook. But there are some powerful principles here. What truths do you see about the process of seeking a godly and loving mate? _____

_____

_____

2. Remember that in our culture the process of dating is meant to lead eventually to marriage. What characteristics do you think are important to look for in someone whom you might choose to spend your life with? _____

_____

_____

WEDNESDAY

Lose Some, Win Some

At the theater, everyone piled out. Drew watched with dismay as the teacher made everyone get off in order, first rows first. "So much for sitting with Michelle and Cheryl," he said to Curt.

"You win some, you lose some," Curt answered with a shrug.

As the girls hurried off the bus, Michelle stopped just outside the door to the right. "I've got to pull up my pantyhose," she said.

Cheryl grinned. "You mean you've got to snag somebody in the back of the bus."

Michelle chuckled. "We'll find out what this clod is made of yet."

Drew and Curt stepped out of the bus, ready to head for the doors. Suddenly he heard a girl's voice to his right. It was Cheryl.

"Curt! Hey, Curt!"

Curt and Drew whipped around. Curt walked over to Cheryl, grinning. Drew didn't move until Curt motioned him over.

"Just wondering if you're sitting with anyone?" Cheryl said coyly.

"I don't know. You have someone in mind?"

Cheryl shrugged. "Beats me. By the way, who's your friend?"

Curt turned to Drew. "This is Drew Hostetter." Drew smiled. He felt uncomfortable, but he couldn't keep several glances from straying to Michelle's eyes.

Cheryl introduced Michelle to both. "She moved here from Harrisburg."

Michelle smiled. Curt said, "So why don't we all sit together?"

They began walking in a clump toward the big wooden doors of the theater where most of the students were gathered. However, Curt edged Drew away from Michelle, putting him next to Cheryl. He engaged Michelle in conversation and it was soon clear who was pairing up with whom.

When they got inside, Drew whispered to Curt, "Hey, what gives? I thought I was supposed to sit with . . ."

"You do your thing and I'll do mine," Curt said briskly. He led Michelle to a seat and Drew followed them with Cheryl, silently fuming.

Perfect Harmony

There's an old proverb about love. It goes like this: "All's fair in love and war."

How true. And how your friends show their real colors when it comes to dating. If two guys get interested in the same girl, a rivalry can spring up that can destroy the friendship. Think of all the grand larcenies done in the name of love, from the love triangle in *Gone with the Wind* (Scarlett O'Hara, Ashley Wilkes, and Rhett Butler) to the *Star Wars* saga of Princess Leia, Luke Skywalker, and Han Solo, multitudes of friends have parted, fought, killed, and died over love. How does one handle it?

Frankly, there's only one way: with gentlemanly and ladylike kindness, understanding, and fortitude. If you're interested in someone, go for it. No one else but you can make it happen. True, God may be all for it, but we have to make the phone call, send the roses, and pick up the tab.

What *is* wrong is using people. Christians are to "love their neighbors as themselves" and "honor one another." There's no place for female cat fights or male gang-wars in the name of love. While Ulysses fought Paris over Helen of Troy, true love needn't end in bloodshed. Or insults. Or broken friendships.

It's a difficult matter. There is no fine line to follow. While there's nothing wrong with a little friendly rivalry, Scripture calls us to show respect, give honor, be open-minded, and serve. What's the balance? I don't know. You'll have to find that one for yourself.

Fine Tunin'

1. Have you ever had a rivalry with someone over the love of another? What was your response—to give in, to fight, to provoke a confrontation, to slink off and hang it up? The fact is that if you value someone's love, you can best show it by giving them all you have. Read what David was willing to do to gain Michal's hand in 1 Samuel 18:17-30. _____

_____

_____

2. In the long run, don't worry about rivalries. They have a way of working themselves out. Until the "I do" anyone is fair game. Meditate on Proverbs 18:22.

THURSDAY

A Little Switch

The play wasn't bad, though the language was a bit too Shakespearean for Drew. He got lost several times. Cheryl was cordial and pretty. But he wasn't interested in her. Michelle and Curt seemed absorbed in one another. After they returned to the bus, though, Curt took the lead with Michelle behind him. Drew saw his chance. He swallowed the pounding in his throat, caught Michelle, and said, "You want to sit together on the bus?"

As she turned around, it seemed a hundred years passed and he felt as if he'd aged all the way to his toes. She said, "I don't have a standing agreement with Curt about it."

Drew laughed, turned to Cheryl, and said, "I think I'll sit with Michelle on the way back." Michelle gave Cheryl a little shrug. Drew and Michelle took a cozy seat in the front. Curt didn't realize what had happened till he'd reached the back.

After the bus episode, Drew thought it would be easier. The ice was broken. Michelle appeared to like him. However, he failed to get her phone number, or even promise to call her. When they parted at the school parking lot where the parents were lined up three deep in their cars, he simply said, "See you in school."

Michelle didn't appear disappointed. She waved to him as she jumped into her father's car.

Drew knew he had to make a move once he got home. He'd asked girls out before and gone out on dates, but only because he needed a date. He hadn't cared that much whether they answered yes or no.

Somehow Michelle was special. He didn't want to blow it. As the days sped on, it seemed to become only more difficult. When he passed her in the hall, she always said hi, but nothing more. More than once he spotted her talking to Dave Barrack and each time his heart drooped.

One night he attempted to get up the courage to call her. But each time he started toward the phone, a rushing sound filled his ears, he froze, and all he could hear were the words, "I'm sorry, Drew. I'm going with Dave Barrack."

Still, he fought off the feelings. "What's so tough about calling the girl up?" he said between gritted teeth.

Finally, he punched the numbers on the princess phone on the bedstand. A woman answered, but it wasn't Michelle.

"Yes? This is the Pellegrino's."

"Uh, um, uh, I mean . . ."

"Yes?"

"Is Michelle there?"

He heard the voice call, "Michelle, it's some boy." A moment later, Michelle's husky voice came on. "This is Michelle."

Drew froze. He needed to go to the bathroom. Somehow he managed, "This is Drew Hostetter."

"Oh, hi Drew."

Silence.

Suddenly Drew realized he hadn't even planned what he was going to say. It all came out in a rush. "I was thinking . . . I mean, I was hoping . . . that is . . . uh, yeah, well . . ." His brain screamed, *Get it together, nerdball!* Finally he squeezed the words out. "I thought you might like to go to a movie or something."

There was no pause. The voice sounded so serene he

wondered if they were on a cloud. "I'd love to. When do you have in mind?"

Drew's brain seemed to pop. *She'd love to! When did I have in mind?* He had no idea.

Perfect Harmony ♪

Until a couple has begun dating regularly, the first few contacts are tenuous at best and nerve-racking at worst. You never know when they might say, "No, it's over buddio!"

But there are a few things to keep in mind when you decide to take the plunge.

One, plan what you're going to say before you make the call. This goes mainly for guys, but girls can rehearse a few things in their minds. To be sure, we all get tongue-tied at the last minute and forget everything we've planned. But that's life. Let it roll.

Two, do something together the first time or so that will not force you to be in constant conversation. A movie is good. A dance. A party. A church social. None of us are born conversationalists and the idea of talking for two or three hours straight can give anyone liver spots. It's good to learn to feel comfortable just in one another's presence before having an in-depth discussion about the basketball team, the latest rock group, or the five points of Calvinism.

Three, don't worry if things don't click from the start. Love takes time to nurture. It's like a single bright coal one must fuel before real commitment and love can burst within a heart. It may be that you'll soon find there really is little between you. Then part with no regrets and a smile. But if you don't fall head over heels in love at first sight, remember that's the stuff of Hollywood, not reality.

There's a great scene in the wonderful movie *Fiddler*

on the Roof in which Tevye the dairyman realizes that each of his daughters has married for love. He and his own wife never even saw one another before their wedding day. It was a marriage arranged by their parents. But Tevye wonders if real love has ever sprung in his wife, Goldie's, heart, and he asks her, "Do you love me?" She replies with all sorts of oblique evasions of the real issue. But in the end she says, "After twenty-five years . . . I suppose I do." Tevye answers, "And I suppose I love you, too."

Love involves emotion, action, decision, and will. But ultimately, it's a commitment, a choice we make consciously. As John said, "We love because [God] first loved us."

Fine Tunin'

1. Many young Christians are nervous about love. They want it to happen so badly they forget just to enjoy one another. Read Romans 12:9-13 for some insights on real love.

2. Make a list of ways you can show love to the schoolmates and friends around you from Romans 12:9-21. What principles can you apply that will show genuine Christian love to those you might like to date? _____

_____

_____

FRIDAY

The Arm Thing

Drew managed to come up with a movie he'd read about. Since he couldn't drive, his mother had to take them. Michelle was lovely when he picked her up. She had pulled her hair back in a French curl. Perfume electrified the air in the car. Glinting earrings accented her ears.

They took their seats in the movie. He helped her off with her coat, then settled down in the bouncy seats, even though he sat stiff and staring ahead.

He managed, "Would you like some popcorn?"

"No, that's okay."

"A coke or anything?"

"No, I'm not really hungry. Maybe later."

His mind screamed, *Say something intelligent, doofus-brain. She's going to think you're a major bozo.* "Have you seen this movie before?"

She laughed. "No, I haven't."

A preview came on. Michelle seemed calm, but the only thing on his mind was whether he should put his arm around her or not. He couldn't think of a single strategy to get it there. And what if she didn't like it? He imagined the conversation:

What are you doing with your arm, Drew?
Oh, I was just stretching it.
Well, stretch it in the other direction.

Or maybe she would sit there stiff and afraid. Maybe she'd think he was trying to pull a move on her. She wouldn't say anything, but it would be clear: Get your slimy hands off me, buster.

Sweat poured into his armpits. Now he was afraid he smelled. He tried to detect if there was a problem. But he knew he couldn't give them a quick sniff.

Then he wondered if he had bad breath. *Did I brush my teeth?* he worried with terror. He licked his teeth, trying to feel for the stench.

The movie began. Michelle seemed to be watching it. But Drew didn't even know what was happening. How was he going to get that arm around her shoulders?

Then it hit him. *Why not just do it, stupid? The worst that can happen is for her to put it back.*

So he did it. Immediately, she cuddled against his shoulder, smiling. He felt her warmth. Now he knew he was in love.

Perfect Harmony

Ah, romance. Such a beautiful thing. Never knock it. Romance is a part of real love, from beginning to end. Girl meeting boy and boy kissing girl are two of the great moments in any young or old lover's life.

But how do you make romance happen?

Frankly, you can't. It's in the chemistry of the situation. Every human has his or her own approach to romance and it's when two romantics find a blend that works for them that the sparks really fly. Yet there are some pointers which any old romantic, such as myself, might offer.

Relax. If it doesn't happen, don't sweat it. You can set the scene, buy the right cologne or perfume, and memorize all the lines. But if you're too tense it won't happen as naturally and beautifully as you would like.

Even though lovers sometimes spot one another "across a crowded room," real romance calls for intimacy.

You want to share it only with the one you love not the gawking gallery.

Have a little pure fun. Be moral. Be biblical. But also, get excited and enjoy one another.

Fine Tunin'

1. Look at these passages on the subject of sex: Galatians 5:19-21, 1 Corinthians 6:9-10, 1 Corinthians 7:1-5, Proverbs 5:1-23, and 6:20-35. What principles can you spotlight from these texts? _____

_____

_____

2. Come up with a list of principles about how you will conduct yourself in a dating relationship. Discuss them with your parents and/or your youth pastor. Once you are sure what you believe in this area, proceed with caution and joy.

WEEKEND

The Main Event

On the way back in the car with Drew's mother driving, the three of them talked about the movie. Michelle was convinced everything had gone so incredibly well, she felt almost high. But she wondered what Drew would do at the door. Would he kiss her good night?

Drew had his arm draped on the seat behind her, but she told herself not to be concerned if he didn't kiss her. This was a good start, even though that might be a good end to the evening.

♪

The whole ride home, all Drew could think about was the door. He'd kissed girls before—at parties where they'd played games and it was more or less meaningless. This was worse than the arm maneuver. How did you approach it? What if Michelle's mother or father walked in just as he planted his lips on hers? What if his lips were too wet? What if they were too dry? What if he had bad breath?

The possibilities seemed staggering. How did anyone get through this?

♪

Drew walked Michelle to the door. The air seemed alive with her scent. In the moonlight, her silky hair shone, and her eyes looked dark, dreamy. He half wondered if he hadn't landed on another planet.

Michelle fumbled with her keys. "You can come inside a moment, if you want."

He said, "Sure."

She opened the door. No one was in sight. It was past eleven o'clock. She turned around to face him. He eased the door slightly shut so his mother wouldn't see what happened, if anything. He didn't want her to know, either way.

Michelle looked up at him. He was at least three inches taller than her, even in heels. "I had a great time, Drew."

He nodded. "Yeah, I enjoyed it."

"I liked the movie a lot."

He swallowed. "Yeah, it was all right." In his mind he screamed, *What do I do? What on earth do I do?*

She said, "Do you want a bite to eat?"

He took a deep breath. "No, my Mom's waiting."

"Oh."

"Well, uh. . . ." Then it came to him. "Michelle, I'd like to kiss . . ."

Without a pause, they came together in a taut, thrilling embrace. Her lips were soft, her breath like a May night. He felt himself sinking into the beauty of it, when suddenly he heard a man's voice behind him. "Hey, what's going on here?"

Both of them pulled apart.

"Daddy!" Michelle cried.

"I'd better go," Drew said quickly. "Good night Michelle. Good night, Mr. Pellegrino."

Michelle said, "Good night." Mr. Pellegrino grunted.

Drew hurried out the door, his heart resounding like a drum roll.

♪

Michelle marched her father into the den. "Mother, don't ever let Daddy do that to me again!"

Her mother rolled her eyes. "I'm sorry, honey. I think he is as embarrassed as you are."

Mr. Pellegrino grinned sheepishly. "Sorry, I didn't know what to say."

Michelle shook her head. "You probably scared him off forever."

But he hadn't. Drew called her up the next day for their next date. Michelle said to herself after she hung up, "Christmas dance, here we come."

Perfect Harmony

Every dating relationship has its funny and memorable moments. Something like the situation above happened to me in my first love relationship on our first date. My girlfriend's father almost did scare me away. But the lure of romance and love kept me coming back.

Remember even the best relationships have their embarrassing moments. But that's the stuff of life.

Remember also that the things that destroy dating relationships are not the little embarrassing moments like the one above. Rather it's distrust, lying, immorality and impurity, gossip, boasting, and many of the falsehoods and intimacies shared in little circles in the locker room. Real intimacy with another person means keeping sacred and private the joys and loves you share. Strive not to sin against one another, but if you do, confess it and apologize. Seek to obey the Lord in all you do and you will find him blessing your friendship, even if it goes no further than a few dates.

Fine Tunin'

1. If you're ready for a big assignment, read The Song of Songs. It's the greatest love story of all time. Using it as

a picture of true love, what truths do you see that you might like to apply in your own dating relationships? ____

_____

_____

 2. How about a date? Why not take that first step—if that's where you are—today? Call up someone and ask her out (if you're a guy). And if you're a girl, you have ways of communicating your desires, too. So why not begin today?

WEEK THREE

Out of Sync and Out of Tune

"IT'S CALLED A 'WOOFAPHONE'. YOUR FATHER
MADE IT IN THE BASEMENT ESPECIALLY
FOR YOU AND HE'S GOING TO BE VERY HURT
IF YOU DON'T PLAY IT TOMORROW
IN THE ORCHESTRA CONCERT."

I've Had It!

"I've had it! You're sixteen. You're supposed to act like a responsible person. And this is not responsible." Lynn Dexter's mother began clearing the kitchen table. To Lynn she appeared stressed and upset for no reason. But before Lynn could answer, her mother swung around and gazed at her with accusing you-never-help-me-out eyes.

"Just consider what people at church would think! I refuse to discuss this any further. Your father will never allow it. And neither will I."

"It's just a weekend, Mother," Lynn said, fighting back her anger. Her mother never seemed to recognize she knew how to take care of herself with boys. And to bring the church into it! Did the church have to govern everything she did?

She knew her mother grew up in a very legalistic church. Over the last few years, her mother had tried to shed her upbringing, but she seemed to feel guilty about everything.

On the other hand, Lynn's church was far from legalistic. It emphasized much more freedom than she knew her mother was accustomed to. That had been part of the problem. Another part, Lynn knew, was her rebel period a year ago. She'd shaved half her head, taken to wearing black all the time, and come home drunk twice. It was a short-lived rebellion, but her mother lost her trust in her.

Lynn threw back her auburn hair and waited in the doorway, hoping a pause and a little quiet would get Mom to change. She remembered what a speaker in the youth group had said once, something about giving a gentle answer can calm people down. But her mother sank back down at the kitchen table, stirring her coffee furiously. The morning sunlight cut hard slats of light through the blinds onto the table. "Mother, I'm not going to let Bill or anyone else . . ."

Mrs. Dexter turned and fixed her fired-up eyes on Lynn. "You don't know what can happen. And I'm not going to let it happen. A whole weekend at the beach with twenty boys and girls and two chaperons? The Gibsons aren't exactly conservatives from what I've heard."

"They're fine. They don't let the kids drink or—"

"I said no—that's final. I'm sorry, but you're not going. I don't need any more problems than I already have."

Lynn stood in the doorway unable to move. She couldn't believe all her plans with Bill, Janie, and Sam were evaporating in one explosion of motherly anxiety. She said, working to keep her tone under control, "I suppose if it was a church thing, you'd be all rarin' for me to go."

Her mother shook her head, looking down at her coffee. "Lynn, I'm sorry, but I just can't handle this right now. Maybe another time. But not now."

Suddenly, before Lynn thought about it, she swore, then whipped around and stalked from the room just in time to see her mother's eyes flare with anger. But Lynn was gone before Mrs. Dexter had a chance to reprimand her.

Perfect Harmony

Lynn's mother is acting like—dare I say this?—a stubborn teenager. Ever see one? Seriously, have you ever felt that an adult you know sometimes acts worse than some of the kids at school, or down the street, or in your own house?

When we think about perfection, holiness, goodness,

and kindness, many parents couldn't claim to have hit the mark, even though some might try. There's a principle here that we might overlook. It's this: parents are humans, too. That means they're not perfect. They sin. They make mistakes. They fail. Sometimes they don't even apologize. Occasionally they even act as though they were right in doing the wrong they did!

One little girl defined relatives as "people who come to dinner who aren't friends." Have you ever felt that those folks at your home dinner table aren't real friends? Often that's precisely the way it is.

But it doesn't have to stay that way. Even while we're in high school and college we can do a lot to work out our differences and problems with Mom and Dad. Notice that Lynn worked at answering her mother gently even though she felt angry. She held back that stinging word that fired into her brain. That's a little thing, but it goes a long way.

A verse from Romans says, "There is no one righteous, not even one; there is no one who understands. . . . There is no one who does good, not even one" (Romans 3:10-12). Paul wasn't saying we never do anything decent or right. He meant we all make plenty of mistakes. That includes Mom, Dad, me, you, and everyone else. Sometimes we simply need to give one another a break!

Fine Tunin'

1. What did Lynn do right in responding to her mother? What other ways might she have responded—right or wrong? _____

_____

2. Look up Proverbs 15:1. Think through two recent situations in which your mom or dad refused to let you do

something you wanted to do. How did you react? What does this proverb suggest about your conduct in future confrontations? _____

_____

_____

TUESDAY

A Friend's Advice

An hour later, Janie's voice urged into the phone, "Just leave, Lynn. You don't have to put up with this."

Lynn bit her lip and stifled her angry tears. "Let's go for a ride or something—I want outta here."

"I'm there."

Fifteen minutes later, Janie pulled up in her mother's Nova and the two girls drove out onto the Interstate. With the windows rolled down, Lynn's hair whipped behind her. The breeze stilled her raging emotions.

"How come you get along with your mom so well, Janie?" she shouted over the roar. "Seems me and my mom can't exchange a word without coming to blows."

Janie laughed. If anything, Janie was a carefree, let-it-all-hang-loose kind of person who never seemed to crumble under problems. Even when her mother struggled through several bouts with cancer, Janie stayed "up."

"You think we get along?" Janie said with a chuckle. "More like we just ignore one another. My parents don't know anything I do, and they don't care. That's fine by me."

Lynn tried to picture Janie's parents not caring. It didn't seem possible. They went to one of the so-called "liberal" churches but she knew they were very involved.

"I don't think they don't care," Lynn said.

Janie smiled. Her blond hair riffled in the air. Lynn envied her coy smile and perfect complexion. "Oh, I know they care. But they found out they couldn't control me. So we have an understanding."

"Oh, yeah, what's that? You never told me."

"I don't smoke, drink, or get pregnant, and they let me do what I want."

"But you . . ."

Janie winked and slowed down to turn off on Rutgers Avenue where the McDonald's was located. Many of their friends hung out around there during the summer and fall. "Yeah, well, for all intents and purposes, I don't do any of that."

Janie had encouraged Lynn many times to smoke and drink, but after a couple tries, Lynn had stopped. Even if her parents didn't trust her, she'd seen enough drunk driving films and lung cancer pictures in school to give her the courage to refuse. Moreover, she did want to live a Christian life, even if at times it seemed difficult.

"So what do you think I should do?"

Janie turned the car into McDonald's and whooped as she spotted Sam's four-by-four. "Looks like we'll get a free Coke, anyway," she said.

A few minutes later, Sam morosely listened to Lynn's story. "Bill's gonna be ripped," he said with finality.

"No, he won't," Lynn said, squelching her doubts. Bill was usually understanding about these things. But she knew he wouldn't be happy. She asked Sam not to say anything until she told Bill in person. Janie and Sam promised.

Perfect Harmony

Maybe you've heard the story about the old man who reached his hundredth birthday. When asked how he'd survived so long, he said, "Well, when Maggie and me got married, we agreed that whenever we had an argument, whoever lost would go for a long walk to think it out. The secret of my health is how much time I've spent over the years in the great outdoors."

♪

Sometimes, quite frankly, the best thing to do when you're upset or angry is to go for a walk or a drive. It's often better to bite your tongue, still your fire, and take a hike than to unleash a flaming paragraph sure to singe everyone in sight.

Still, it's hard. When people make unreasonable demands, especially our parents, we prefer to let them have it. It might be better to sit tight and wait it out.

Notice that Lynn sought Janie's counsel about the problem. Never discount the advice of a good friend, even if they don't happen to be Christians. You can always choose not to apply the advice when they suggest something you don't agree with. But more importantly, simply telling your story to a sympathetic person helps. Lynn's mom is acting unreasonable and tense. Blasting away with verbal dynamite would only make things worse. Solomon, the wisest man who ever lived, said that there is wisdom in many counselors (see Proverbs 11:14). Undoubtedly, he sought advice before taking action with one of his seven hundred wives!

When you have trouble with a parent, before you make a decision about what to do, think about talking to a friend, pastor, or even the other parent. You might be surprised—not only by what they say, but by how much better it makes you feel. The world always looks less terrible once you've talked to someone about it.

Fine Tunin'

1. Janie didn't offer Lynn much insight into the problem. What do you see that she did by way of help? __

_____

_____

2. How important to you are friends you can confide

in? Notice how David dealt with his problem with King Saul in 1 Samuel 20:1-42. Comment on his relationship with Jonathan and how they helped each other. _____

_____

_____

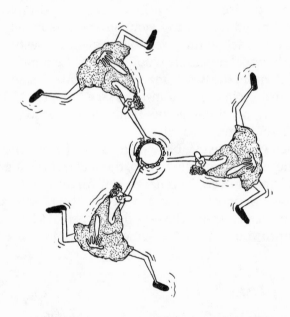

WEDNESDAY

Walk Softly

When Lynn met Bill during his short break while working at Hess's Lawn and Garden, he wasn't angry and quickly decided to stay home. "We'll go out on our own," he said. "We don't need some old beach party to have fun."

Lynn hoped this would be his response and stroked his hand playfully. He always came up with an alternative to her mom's staunch rejections of things like this. "We can hit a movie or something."

"Just as long as it isn't rated R," Lynn said with a roll of her eyes.

Bill put his arm over her shoulder. "Hey, don't sweat it. We can go where we want. Maybe we'll just look at the moon for awhile down at Saunder's Bend."

Lynn smiled as she thought about the times without number that Bill had romanced her down there. One thing about Bill, she knew, was that she felt safe with him. Both about things like sex and also plain compassion and understanding. He never raged like Sam did when a big plan fizzled. Her parents' approval of him from the start almost kept her from dating him. He'd become a Christian the year before. In fact, his whole family turned to faith. And now his commitment to God helped her in her own struggles with faith.

That night, Bill came over and they cruised around in his father's Thunderbird. Lynn nestled next to him and laid her head on his shoulder, giving his right ear a quick kiss. As they drove around with the sun roof open, she looked out at the stars and said, "What do you do when your parents put a leash on you, Billy-boy? You seem to get along pretty well."

He stroked her knee and said, "Ah, they were skeptical about letting me go to this beach thing, too—for your information. It made it a little easier to decide when you couldn't go."

Lynn jerked up. "You're kidding."

He smiled, then put his arm over her shoulders, hugging her. "No, they wanted me to go actually. They said they trusted me and wanted me to have a witness with my friends."

"Come on."

He laughed. "Well, I thought of that part. Even told them. They liked the idea. I think they figure since we became Christians last year everything will work out."

"But they don't."

"Yeah, well, it's better than it was."

"But what about when you really disagree about things?"

Bill gave her a reflective look with his dark blue eyes. Lynn loved his thick eyebrows and curly brown hair. "I'll have to think about that one. But basically I just try to listen to what they say. You know, walk softly, but carry a big argument."

Lynn laughed. She liked the way Bill was always twisting around some famous quote.

Perfect Harmony ♪

It's encouraging to have a sympathetic boyfriend or girlfriend. Not all who read this book are dating someone, but often a friend of the opposite sex can also help. Clearly, Bill was understanding and winsome in his comments to Lynn. He did offer an uplifting insight, too: Walk softly, but carry a big argument. How does that sound to you by way of advice?

We often screech about an injustice, then forget the power of simple persuasion. "A gentle answer turns away wrath," as Solomon said.

Suppose you want to attend a beach party like Lynn did and Mom is against it. Wouldn't it be wise to think through a straightforward and honest statement to attempt to persuade her to your point of view? Granted, you ultimately have to obey your parents' final decree. But sometimes when you offer valid light on the subject, you can win them over. Raving only throws up a brick wall.

The old maxim, "More flies are caught with honey than vinegar," stands. We all make progress by being kind and compelling rather than insulting.

Fine Tunin'

1. Think through the last time you had a disagreement with your parents. Did you make an honest effort to listen to them? Did you try to persuade them—rationally, not emotionally—to your point of view? How might you go about it differently? _____

_____

_____

2. Read Proverbs 18:21. How can you begin using your tongue for life and not death in your relationship with your parents? _____

_____

_____

THURSDAY

Totally Unreasonable

"How would you like to go horseback riding at my grandmother's?" Lynn asked Bill over the phone the next day. "She called and invited me down for Saturday. I know my mother won't be against that."

"Sure. We haven't done that since the beginning of the summer. I'll let my mom and dad know right away and make sure I can get the car."

"The Thunderbird?"

"If I can."

Friday night, Lynn's mother was in a bad mood and almost put the brakes on her visit to her grandmother's. Her father was late getting home from work as usual. He didn't want to deal with his wife's criticism and had become more and more distant, staying away. Lynn knew he'd had an affair—years ago—but it had struck division and unhappiness in her family now for over ten years.

Mrs. Dexter paced and drank coffee. Then Bill called and said he couldn't get the car for Saturday. His father had work to do and his mother needed the station wagon all day for errands. He asked, "You think your mom would let me drive one of your cars?"

Lynn took a deep breath. Her father had allowed Bill to drive his car twice before. But he wasn't home right now and Bill wanted to know right away. "I'll tell you later. Maybe I can ask my dad first."

She called her father's work number, but there was no answer. She knew she should probably wait, but there wasn't much time. Her mother sat in an easy chair trying to read a book when Lynn approached her. It was past eight o'clock. Lynn explained calmly what she needed.

"Lynn, I have a horde of things to do tomorrow. Please understand, but you can't take my car."

"Well, what about Dad's?"

"I can't answer for him. You'll just have to wait. But I know he was planning to go into the office tomorrow. You know he's been traveling all week."

Lynn tried to think of some way to get what she wanted. "Please, Mom, we . . ."

Her mother sighed heavily. "Lynn, I don't feel very good. I'm very upset about some things and I want to be alone. Don't fight me on this—you have my answer."

Lynn took a deep breath. She knew her mother had been running all week with taking her brothers to games, church activities, and some problems about house insurance. But it still made her mad. Her mother wasn't even willing to meet her halfway. She hesitated to dial Bill's number, but finally she did. As always, he shook it off. "We'll take a long walk in the trees and the breeze," he said. His response made it easier, but she had been looking forward to the horseback riding.

Finally, she called her grandmother and explained. Gram responded, "How 'bout if Granddad and I come in and pick you up? It's only an hour drive and you can stay over Sunday. Your friend can sleep in the guest room and you can go in your mom's old room."

Lynn hadn't even thought of this, and she exclaimed, "Oh, would you, Gram?"

"Sure. Now that Granddad's retired we need some youngsters to get the juices flowing."

"Great. I'll tell Bill and Mom."

Lynn's mother's first words were, "You're making your grandparents come all the way down here just to pick you up?"

Lynn crushed the rising anger within her, and said, "Mom, Gram volunteered."

Mrs. Dexter gave her a penetrating look. "I'll bet."

Lynn threw up her hands in anger. "Don't you ever trust me about anything?"

"Well, I'll just call Mother and see what she says."

Lynn listened with folded arms and a sarcastic, I-told-you-so grimace as her grandmother assured her mother about Saturday. Then her mom tried to talk Gram out of it, saying that Lynn shouldn't impose. But obviously Gram didn't feel that way. When her mother put down the phone, she said, "Okay, I was wrong," then went back to her chair.

Lynn left the room with clenched teeth, but when she called Bill and told him what was up, he calmed her down. "Maybe your mom's had a bad week, Lynn. She probably thinks you think the whole world revolves around you."

"Whose side are you on?"

"Yours, but you're not going to get anywhere by constantly fighting. Try to see what she's thinking or feeling at least. Don't you think?"

"I guess so."

"Hang in there, Babe. Things aren't so bad. You've got me."

Lynn rolled her eyes, but she said, "It better stay that way, too, or I'll go nuts."

Bill's voice took on his quiet, earnest tone. "You've always got me, girl."

Lynn's throat knotted, but she hung up saying, "Thanks for hanging with me, Bill."

"Anytime."

Perfect Harmony

Lynn's mother is on edge most of the time and appears insensitive to Lynn's needs. She is preoccupied with her own problems and doesn't have the energy to listen to her daughter. She takes a position and then refuses to budge.

Are your parents like that? How do you respond to them? Fly off the handle? Scream, shout, and stomp about? Put out a contract?

Lynn is frustrated, understandably. Her boyfriend is supportive, but she's in a tough spot. A home with problems is never easy. When Mom and Dad are in bad straits it affects the kids in all sorts of ways.

But maybe we're missing something important here: Lynn's mother. All right, she's not very nice. But why is she that way? Could Lynn make an effort to understand her better? Jesus said, "Blessed are the merciful, for they will be shown mercy" (Matthew 5:7). Just as sons and daughters need mercy from parents, so parents occasionally require mercy from their children.

Often the key to a good relationship is not pushing and shoving to get your own way, but stepping back and trying to understand why a person—even a parent—won't budge. Ask yourself: Did I just catch them in a bad mood, or is there something under the surface I'm not seeing, another problem hidden beneath the smoldering emotions?

Clearly, Lynn's mother faced her own deep difficulties: a husband who had an affair. Since he's coming home late, she's probably worried he might be doing it again. She also has a legalistic conscience from her youth and a daughter who had already gone through one very rebellious period. Realizing how her mother must be feeling could help Lynn be more understanding.

Fine Tunin'

1. What might Lynn do to try to understand her mom? Do you think she might be so wrapped up in her world that she has forgotten her mother has feelings, too? What can she do to reach out? _____

_____

_____

2. Read Matthew 5:3-9. What qualities do you see listed here which might help Lynn in her relationship with her mother? _____

_____

_____

FRIDAY

Gram's Opinion

Gram helped Lynn and Bill get the gray stallion, Custer, and Sitting Bull, a dappled quarter horse, ready on Saturday. They rode off with a picnic lunch in Lynn's saddlebag. Together, they cantered down a trail in the woods, then galloped on the paths through the fields spotted with dandelions and purple bits of alfalfa and the first green shoots of stray wheat. A slight breeze tugged at her ponytail and made her feel fresh and new and alive.

Lynn had forgotten how much she enjoyed riding. Granddad had given her Custer when she was twelve and until she was fifteen, she went out nearly every weekend to groom him and ride. But the last year she'd lost interest. Bill had taken Custer's place in her heart. She knew Gram noticed, but Gram always nodded and said, "Growing up, that's all. We like taking care of him anyway."

Then that night, Bill went off to inspect Granddad's woodwork in the barn. Gram and Lynn sat drinking Cokes and chuckling over past times. Lynn kept thinking of her mother and how bad their relationship was. She'd always been able to talk to Gram. After several minutes of small talk, she said, "Gram, I can't seem to get along with Mom for anything. We argue about everything."

Gram smiled. She kept her hair curly with a light gray tint. But Lynn knew from pictures she'd been a ravishing blonde as a girl. "As if it had been any different when she was my kid and you were just a gleam in your father's eye."

"You and Mom argued a lot?"

"We still do, or haven't you noticed?"

79

"Well, I guess—now that I think about it."

Gram brushed Lynn's hair affectionately. "Lynn, you have to work at it. No magician will step in, wave his wand, and make everything perfect. You have to trust God, I know, but he didn't make this world the same as the world to be. Here, things are hard—especially relationships."

Lynn sipped her Coke thoughtfully. "What do you mean 'work at it'?"

Gram laughed with a gentle snort. "You have to decide you're going to make things go, that's all. Work. Be patient, try to talk about what's happening, work at trying to understand her viewpoints. That's all. Just decide you'll love her. You can't change her. But you can change you."

Lynn was silent.

"Keep trying," Gram said again. "Don't give up. And the Lord'll do something. God never closes a door where He doesn't also open a window somewhere. Your mom's going through a hard time. Ever since your dad . . . well . . ." She didn't finish the sentence.

"I know, Gram. But Dad has tried, really tried."

Gram nodded. "Just keep your chin up, honey. You may have to help her keep her's up, too."

Lynn gazed at her grandmother with amazement. "Keep her's up?"

"She thinks your Dad doesn't love her anymore. She thinks he might be having an affair again. He's all wound up with his job. I really don't know how serious this is yet. But you'll have to be patient, whatever comes."

Lynn sighed. "Easy for you to say."

Gram winked and sipped her Coke. "It'll be all right. You'll see." Bill and Granddad came in a moment later, and everyone settled down to a brisk game of Monopoly.

Perfect Harmony

Sometimes grandparents can be the greatest friends you have in this world. They not only want to listen to you, they will drive miles to give you the chance to talk! Wisdom does come with age, too. The perspective of years enables a loving grandparent to help us in ways others can't.

Proverbs says, "Gray hair is a crown of splendor; it is attained by a righteous life" (Proverbs 16:31). Solomon meant that people who live righteous lives live much longer than sinners. You can be sure that many of those with gray heads have learned how to live decent, clean, and wise lives. Not always. Just most of the time. (Maybe not even most of the time. It's just a proverb!)

Just the same, Lynn wasn't alone. She had friends and relatives to help, though in many cases grandparents live thousands of miles away. It's unfortunate that in our world the extended family is extended all the way to the North Pole.

Moreover, Lynn did have control over one person: herself. While she couldn't change her mother, she could still control her own actions and responses. One of the most important things we as Christians must remember is that while we can't change others, under God's power and direction we can be changed ourselves. Sometimes that's the best we can hope for in a world so filled with evil. That's why staying close to God is so important. He alone promises to go through the valley of the shadow with us.

Anne Lindbergh once wrote, "It is not physical solitude that actually separates one from other men, not physical isolation, but spiritual isolation. It is not the desert island, not the stony wilderness that cuts you from the people you love. It is the wilderness in the mind, the desert wastes in the heart through which one wanders lost and a stranger."[1]

Friday

We are most alone when we withdraw within ourselves spiritually. Fortunately, Lynn did not do that. Her grandmother proved the key piece of wisdom she needed to solve her problem. Notice what Lynn has done so far to find a way to get along with her mother: first, she talked to several friends. Second, she obeyed her mother, even when she didn't like it. Third, she talked about it with her grandmother and listened to her advice. Fourth, she began to break out of her own mindset and take an objective look at her mother.

Those elements are all keys to getting along with your parents. There will always be times when they say, "No way, never, and no how!" Other times they may give in to your pressure, but fume about it inside. Still other times they will be eager and willing to go along with your request. Ultimately, though, there are many ways to work to bring harmony to your home. Remember they have a lot on their minds—like you do. Sometimes they can't hear because of the static on their internal wires.

Don't give up. Relationships, all of them, take effort, persistence, and determination to make them a success. Work at applying the truth to your problem, and God will certainly open up a window.

Fine Tunin' ♪

1. What do you think of Gram's advice? Why is it good or not so good, in your thinking? _____
_____
_____

2. Look at Galatians 6:9-10. What principles can you apply in your relationships from this passage? _____
_____
_____

WEEKEND

God Opens a Window

Gram's words still echoed in Lynn's ears when she got home Sunday night. Dad stayed busy in his little office and Mom ironed and watched a video, so Lynn said little and went to bed early.

Monday morning, when Lynn came down to breakfast, her mother sat in her pink bathrobe at the table, a cup of coffee steaming in her hands. She had the same vacant, tired look on her face. Lynn reminded herself again of Gram's words, then pulled out a box of Raisin Bran, a bowl, and some milk. "How are you feeling, Mom?" she said, trying to be friendly.

Her mother didn't answer.

Lynn sat down and poured the cereal into the pink and white bowl with roses enameled into the surface. She studied the bowl a moment. She'd never noticed the design before in quite this way. She poured the rich white milk onto the brown flakes. "These bowls are pretty, Mom. Where did you get them?"

"What are you, Miss Happy and Hearty, this morning? We've had them for years."

Lynn grimaced, then prayed briefly and dug into the Raisin Bran. "Just trying to be nice, that's all."

"Well, I wouldn't want you to try too hard!"

Lynn shot back in her seat, about to make a raw comment and storm from the room. But she forced back her irritation and gazed directly at her mother. For the first time she noticed how sad her mom's eyes looked. "Mom, I'm just . . ."

Her mother ran her fingers through her hair and looked out the window, avoiding Lynn's eyes.

Lynn breathed in tightly, then began to take another spoonful of cereal. She told herself not to give up. As she stilled her emotions, she slid her hand across to her mother's still gripping her coffee cup. When she touched her hand, her mother flinched, but she didn't pull her hand away. Lynn said quietly, "Mom, I want us to be friends. That's all. Just friends. We used to be. Can't we try again?"

Mrs. Dexter didn't move her hand for what seemed a minute. She stared at the cup, saying nothing. Lynn wondered what to do. She resisted the impulse to pull her hand away.

Her mother looked up and sighed. "I guess I'd forgotten what it was like."

"What?"

She pulled her hand away nervously and drank from the cup. "For us to talk."

Lynn swallowed. "Maybe we should try harder."

Her mother gazed at her then flinched away. "Yeah, I guess so."

Lynn summoned up her courage to say I love you, but she wasn't sure how her mother would respond. She decided to talk about the weather.

Mom stood up and walked over to the window, then turned around. "I'm sorry, Lynn."

"For what?"

"I don't know. I'm just sorry. Can we start there?"

Lynn nodded. She realized there was a lot of hidden pain in her mother's life. She thought maybe just talking in a friendly way would help. They talked for a few more minutes about some news events and Lynn's plans for the day. Lynn noticed, though, that her mother made no sarcastic comments. Maybe Gram was right. There was no magic wand that could be waved over a relationship to make it work. But maybe God had opened that window, if only a crack.

Perfect Harmony

I once heard a story about a mother, father, and young daughter in a restaurant. When the girl's mother ordered her a hamburger, she specifically said, "No onions, please." The little girl protested, "But I want onions." The waitress took the order without comment. But when the hamburger came, to the little one's delight, there were onions on it. As the waitress walked away, the girl exclaimed triumphantly, "She thinks I'm real!"

Just as parents sometimes treat their children as "unreal" or "like we don't exist," so teenagers can respond in kind to their parents. The real breakthrough in Lynn's situation occurred when she decided to befriend her mother even though the latter was obstinate and downright nasty. One of the great principles that comes with being a Christian is that we all must learn to do right regardless of what others do. We're responsible before God for our own conduct, even if the whole world goes the other way!

On the night of January 30, 1956, as Dr. Martin Luther King, Jr. spoke in a Baptist church, a radical group bombed his house. His wife and ten-month old baby escaped by chance. Later that night, over a thousand angry followers assembled on King's lawn, ready for war with guns, knives, clubs, and broken bottles. How would Dr. King respond at this most pivotal of moments?

He appeared on the porch and said to the crowd, "If you have weapons, take them home. If you do not have them, please do not seek to get them. We cannot solve this problem through retaliatory violence. . . . We must make them know that we love them. Jesus still cries out in words that echo across the centuries: 'Love your enemies; bless them that curse you; pray for them that despitefully use you.' This is what we must live by. We must meet hate with love."[2]

Dr. King's words still resound today. "We must meet hate with love"—even if that hate, anger, or nastiness comes from your own parents. When we practice that brand of love, everything is possible.

Fine Tunin'

1. Read 1 Corinthians 13:4-8 and put yourself in Lynn's situation. What ways might she have loved her mother according to Paul's instructions? _____

_____

_____

2. Do you feel you have unreasonable parents? Why not take the step of deciding to love them—come hell or high water—from this day forward? What good might it accomplish in them—and you? _____

_____

_____

Notes

1. Anne Morrow Lindbergh, *Gift from the Sea* (New York: Pantheon, 1975), 44.

2. Milton Viorst, *Fire in the Streets* (New York: Simon and Schuster, 1980), 40.

WEEK FOUR

Time to Face the Music

IT WASN'T ENOUGH TO BE A GOOD MUSICIAN. TO MAKE IT ON THE MILBURN HIGH ALL-TERRAIN MARCHING BAND YOU ALSO HAD TO HAVE STRENGTH, SPEED, AGILITY, AND DETERMINATION.

MONDAY

.414 Season

David Ambler bent over the stats once again.[1] "I can't believe it," he murmured. "I batted .414 this year."

He had already checked the figures twice. When the team trainer first rushed in to tell him, he was skeptical. Apparently, several early games had mistakenly been overlooked in the original tabulations. But now he was convinced. "Pittsburgh Pirates, here I come," he said to himself. "It's a cinch. Just keep hitting like this in college and I'm home free." He'd already won MVP for senior year in high school and a pro scout had seen him hit in two games.

David laid back in his dad's desk chair and laughed. "I ought to go for it now," he mused. "Forget college. That would be the greatest heist of all. I can see the headlines. 'Ambler makes it out of the minors in the first week of the season!' "

As David daydreamed, he became drowsy. His eyelids sagged. In moments he was snoring in the burgundy leather chair, as unassuming and relaxed as a sparrow on a guy line.

Then suddenly a sharp sound penetrated his sleep and he jolted awake. After glancing around, he mumbled, "Just the wind. What's gotten into you, David?"

But a strange shadow appeared from behind the curtains and David's heart jumped. "Who's there?" he shouted. "Dad?"

To his alarm a voice answered. "I'm sorry. I wanted to get you while you were still asleep."

David jumped up and pulled open a drawer, grasping his father's revolver. His Dad was a stickler for security and David knew how to use the gun and when. They'd already had one robbery the previous year. He pointed the barrel at the shadow, which was now moving toward him.

"Who are you?" David cried.

"Death," said the voice, quavery and crackly.

Perfect Harmony

Like it or not, we all have to reckon with this kind of moment. How we look at death will determine much of how we live life. Indifference to death spells indifference to morality, truth, goodness, and love. Fear of death leads to fear of nearly everything else, for anything could hurl us into the maw of death—a car accident, a disease, an inner city encounter.

How can we reconcile ourselves with the fact that we all must one day die? Only by accepting the reality of death and reckoning with what it means.

Hollywood has painted a powerful picture of what happens at death. One recent movie pictures a good man dying and coming back to earth as a spirit to help his girlfriend get her life back on track. Another shows several medical students making themselves die to see the other side. But when they come back, past guilts come back to haunt them and until they straighten that out, their lives are havoc. A third shows the good guy who gets murdered having to stay around on earth as a spirit. He finally learns to communicate with his girlfriend through a medium and eventually learns who killed him. When his murderer dies, however, he doesn't get a happy welcome into the great beyond. Instead, demon-like creatures whoosh up out of the ground and carry him off, presumably to some kind of torture chamber.

When we study these ideas, though, we soon find they contradict and disagree with one another. Hollywood's thoughts and cinemascope views are little more than rank speculation. Worse, they're suggestions about what could happen without offering a shred of proof of what actually does happen. A person may take one philosophy to heart, live in light of it, and find out at the end it's little more than a lie in shining video.

I'm not trying to be morbid. However, statistically it's said that most teenagers and adults think about death at least once every five minutes. That's 132 times a day if you're awake sixteen hours. That's far more probably than any other subject we might muse on, except perhaps the person we're in love with at the moment.

I once heard Tony Campolo tell this story. An elderly woman said, "Death is like a stuck organ note. When you're young and free, the note is quiet and low, barely making a sound in the midst of all the beautiful music. As you get older the note grows louder and provokes some joking and honest complaints, but it's still not too troublesome. Then when you reach your fifties and sixties, the note has become downright annoying. And loud. It ruins every piece of music you play. But still, you can learn to play around it and even make the music sing—a little. Nonetheless, when you get into your late sixties and seventies, you begin to hear nothing but that one note. It screams into your consciousness no matter what music you're playing. That to me is death. The nearer I get to it, the more horrible and beckoning it becomes."

Even if you don't feel you think of death a lot, you must decide what you believe before you encounter it. Someone once told me, "Until a person reckons with death, he never is free to really live." Death is all around us, and an honest understanding of it is essential to joyful living. The fear of death and what happens after it forces us to think through what we believe perhaps more than any other factor.

There are many important reasons to trust Christ: so that we can become a part of God's purpose and kingdom; to be delivered from personal sin; to become the kind of people God intended for us to become.

My purpose is not to scare people into believing in Christ. Rather, it's that we all honestly face our mortality, come to our own convictions about the meaning of life, and then begin living in light of them.

Fine Tunin'

1. Read Jesus' words in John 14:1-3 about the future for every believer. Get the context in mind. Jesus was about to die on the cross. The disciples were afraid. But he assured them of a great truth. How do you feel about this truth? Is it real to you, or just a "Christian fantasy?" _____

_____

_____

2. Discuss with a close friend some of your feelings about death. Have you ever lost a relative or close friend? What were your feelings? What did you think? How do you think the truths about Christ can help us face such tragedies? _____

_____

_____

TUESDAY

This Isn't a Dream!

David laughed. "Death! This has got to be a dream. Wake up, you fool."

The shadow moved closer. "I'm sorry, but you are awake, though I had planned to get you while still asleep. I really hate these arguments, you know."

David swallowed. "You mean this is real? I've never heard about anything like this."

The shadow moved as though a head were shaking. "That's why I prefer to get them while they're asleep. Most people complain profusely about it, making threats, screaming, claiming all sorts of things like it's unfair and so forth and so on. Anyway, I wish I could wait, but I have to begin the count now or I'll be late. So if you don't mind, ten, nine . . . "

David backed up as the shadow moved forward. "What are you doing? What do you mean 'count'? Am I about to die?"

"Yes . . . eight, seven—"

"Hold it!" shouted David. His voice echoed and he jumped at its sound. But instantly he returned to the shadow, trying to make out a shape or face. "Look, I don't know what you're doing, but I think I ought to at least have an explanation. What's this all about? I hit .414 this past season."

Death sighed. "It's the way these things are carried out. I simply count you out. It's similar to the thing referees do with boxers, though I know you're a baseball player. Anyway, this is a much more solemn affair and I hate to turn it into a circus. But you see, I have to be precise about these things. The appointments are fixed and precise down to the second, so I'm always very careful to do a count. It helps me keep things on schedule."

David's shoulders slumped as Death spoke. Death's voice chilled him through. It felt like freezing cold on his face. At the same time, it made him sleepy.

Death went on, "Anyway, if you don't mind, I'll continue. Six . . ."

Perfect Harmony

A rather grim picture. Over dramatized no doubt. Yet, consider some of the words of those who came to the precipice of eternity without Christ.

Napoleon Bonaparte, French world conqueror who died in exile said: "I die before my time, and my body will be given back to the earth to become food for worms. Such is the fate of him who has been called the great Napoleon. What an abyss lies between my deep misery and the eternal kingdom of Christ!"[2]

An attendant upon David Hume, a rejecter of Christ, spoke of what she witnessed at his death bed: "He was anything but composed. His mental agitation was so great at times as to occasion his whole bed to shake!"[3]

Now read some of the words of those who faced death with Christ in their hearts.

Elizabeth Barrett Browning, poetess, who once declared, "We want the touch of Christ's hand upon our literature," at the moment of truth, cried, "It is beautiful."[4]

Michelangelo, famed painter and sculptor: "I commit my soul to God, my body to the earth, my possessions to my nearest relatives. I die in the faith of Jesus Christ and in the firm hope of a better life." His final words were,

"Throughout life remember the sufferings of Jesus."[5]

A girl, age ten, named Lillian Lee, lay dying. She told her father, "Oh! Papa, what a sweet sight! The gates are open and crowds of children come pouring out. Oh, such crowds." Later, she said, "They ran up to me and began to kiss me and call me by a new name. I can't remember what it was." Finally, as her eyes closed in death, she seemed to have a vision of Christ, and said, "Yes, yes, I come, I come!"[6]

Mrs. Catherine Booth, wife of William Booth, founder of the Salvation Army: "The waters are rising, but so am I. I am not going under, but over! Do not be concerned about dying—go on living well and the dying will be right."[7]

I'm not trying to scare you. Nor am I saying that being a Christian insures our deaths will be easy, without pain, or even peaceful. It's not always that way. Yet, to those who believe, Christ assures us, "I am the resurrection and the life. He who believes in me will live, even though he dies; and whoever lives and believes in me will never die" (John 11:25-26).

The youth group at my church recently suffered the loss of a fellow student who was killed by a drunk driver in a car accident. Many of the people involved were angry at God, feeling he had been unjust for taking this vibrant and new Christian girl so early in her life. They were all forced to face, for a moment, their own mortality. Many others became Christians as a result.

Still, it wasn't the witness of how she had died that communicated so much. It was the confidence of so many young Christians and their faith in the midst of it that helped.

We must all live with the reality of death. But living through it with triumph can only come to those who are confident they have a Savior who conquered death forever.

Fine Tunin'

1. Read the story of the raising of Lazarus in John 11:1-45. Notice that Jesus chose not to save his friend from death, but to let him die and then resurrect him. Why do you think Jesus might have done this? _____
_____
_____

2. The Christian believes that Jesus rose from the dead and reigns now in heaven. What do you believe happened that Sunday after the crucifixion? Why? What facts do you have to support your idea? _____
_____
_____

WEDNESDAY

Counting Him Out

The number rang out like a shot. David leaped back to full alert. "This isn't right," he seethed. "You have no right. I'm not ready to die. I may be going into pro baseball next year. I've got a great future. I'm not ready to die. You'll have to change your schedule."

Death shook his head with frustration. "What makes you think these things can be changed? It's not as though you're in charge here."

Now David was angry. "This is my dad's office," he said, "and we haven't asked you here. I think you'd better go."

"Five . . ."

David leaped forward at the shadow, trying to grab it. But it seemed to surround him.

"Who do you think you are?" he shouted. "This isn't fair. If you really want to take me, then at least give me notice and several days to think about it."

"It's not done that way," Death said patiently. "I come when I'm told—no sooner, no later. And you don't do the telling."

"Then who does? Tell me that. I'd like to speak to him."

Death sighed again. "You'll be appearing before him soon enough," he said. "Four . . ."

"And who is he—God, I suppose?" David said sarcastically. "Well, I don't believe in him."

"That doesn't matter," said Death. "Personal preferences and ideas about God don't change the fact of who or what he is."

Perfect Harmony

Truth is truth whether we believe it or not. For instance, a person may take a pill composed of cyanide, a deadly poison that kills in seconds. What if he believes the pill is really aspirin? Does that change the fact that it's cyanide? It will kill him just as quickly regardless of his belief.

Similarly, a friend of mine once had a maid who didn't believe American astronauts had landed on the moon. She claimed it was all hyped up and done on television but that no one really made that "one small step for man," and that "one giant step for mankind." She was absolutely sincere and convinced she was right because her pastor said it was so.

But did that make it so?

A humorist once said, "So many people believe so many things that just ain't so!"

Amen. Christianity is one of those faiths that is often ridiculed because we "take it by faith" and we "believe in spite of the facts." The truth is that Christianity is built on powerful and consistent information passed down through the centuries. Scholars have tested and found the Bible precise and exact on numerous issues. It's true there are problems. But problems do not make the Scriptures any less true. It's possible there are a few things we just don't have enough knowledge about. Someone said to Mark Twain, "Doesn't it bother you about all the things in the Bible you don't understand?" Twain replied, "I'm not bothered by what I don't understand in the Bible, but by what I do understand!"

Touché. Peter tells us in his letter, "We did not follow cleverly invented stories when we told you about the power and coming of our Lord Jesus Christ, but we were eyewitnesses of his majesty" (2 Peter 1:16).

Some might accuse Christians of putting their heads in the sand or believing despite the facts, but in reality we believe because of a multitude of solid facts that have held firm for nearly two thousand years. You and I can stake our lives on what the Bible says.

Fine Tunin'

1. Read 2 Peter 1:16-21. What does this passage reveal about the truth of the Scriptures? _____
_____
_____

2. If you have doubts about the truth of the Bible, try reading a book like Josh McDowell's, *More Than a Carpenter* or *Evidence That Demands a Verdict*. God has given us strong reasons to believe in him. It's up to us to find out those reasons. _____
_____
_____

THURSDAY

No Way Out

For a moment David was stunned. Somehow he'd always thought that one's belief or lack of it was the determining factor. But he was angry. He replied, "Well, then he should have informed me about himself. If he's so sure about his existence, why didn't he make me sure?"

Death's voice continued to intone with patience. "Do you have a Bible? Yes, I see it over on the shelf there. Aren't there churches in this neighborhood? Yes, I passed three on this very street. Hasn't your girlfriend repeatedly expressed a desire that you believe in Jesus? Of course. My records show, in fact, that various other relatives, several local pastors, two friends in your school, a player on your team, several people on the street, and numerous others have all mentioned to you the need to believe and follow Christ. In each case, your conscience also reminded you to listen."

David sputtered and shook his head, but Death kept on. "In addition, our records show that over four hundred thousand times—413,674 to be exact—throughout your seventeen years on earth, you were reminded about wrong actions of every sort. In each case, it was recorded that according to principle, your conscience told you that what you were doing was wrong both before, during, and after the acts of sin. It is also written that you only changed your actions under threat of punishment, and that was only in a few cases."

David clenched and unclenched his fist repeatedly on the handle of his pistol. "I suppose you know all about me. Then tell me this, know-it-all. What about when I went forward for baptism in my church when I was twelve? Doesn't that count for anything?"

Death wheezed a lengthy sigh. "The records show that this particular act was motivated by a desire to gain a certain medal in your Boy Scout troop."

"A lie!" shouted David. "You have no proof of that."

"Look," said Death. "I have a long night ahead of me. My responsibility is not to prove anything. That will all be taken care of. I really do have to get on with this. Really, if you had considered that I would come some day you might have been better prepared."

Perfect Harmony

One of the issues many of us worry about is whether those who have never heard of Christ will be punished by God through sending them to hell. The truth is that God has the power to make himself known to each of us in a multitude of ways. If we fear that a person may never hear of Christ, we can rely on the fact that God promises always to deal with all men justly, righteously, and perfectly. We can trust that he will do right by every person who has ever lived.

The truth is that if you are reading this book you may be a prime candidate for faith in Christ. Hopefully, you are already a Christian. But it's always possible you might not be. Paul warned us to "examine [ourselves] to see whether [we] are in the faith" (2 Corinthians 13:5). Peter told us to "be all the more eager to make [our] calling and election sure" (2 Peter 1:10). Everyone of us must take a hard look at ourselves to be sure we're in the faith. We can tell not only by what we believe but by how we live. True believers will want to obey Christ. Even though we will fail and sin at times, the realty of our lives is not that we be sinless but that we sin less and less and less!

Are you sure of your faith in Christ? I hope so. I would not want anyone to read this book and not come away more convinced that Jesus loves them and wants to lead them to glory.

Aaron Burr was Vice President of the United States under Thomas Jefferson from 1801 to 1805. He was also the grandson of Jonathan Edwards, the great New England evangelist who started The Great American Awakening in the early 1700s. Edwards tried repeatedly to get his grandson to believe in Christ. Burr responded that he wanted nothing to do with God and wished simply that God would leave him alone. He preferred advancing his law and political career.

He did achieve some success, but in 1804 he fought a duel with Alexander Hamilton over Hamilton's accusations against his character. He won and Hamilton was killed. In 1807 he was accused of treason. Though it was never proved, he fled to Spain and ultimately returned to the United States, bankrupt, lonely, and rejected. His political career over, he practiced law until his death in 1836. During his last years, he said sadly to a group of friends, "Sixty years ago I told God that if he would let me alone, I would let him alone, and God has not bothered me since."

God gave Burr what he asked for. He died a broken and lost man.

Fine Tunin'

1. Where do you stand with Christ? Read Acts 4:11-12 and 2 Corinthians 5:20-21. If you have not yet become a Christian, try to articulate your reasons for not making that step. _____

_____

2. Read Christ's invitation in John 7:37-39. How do you think these verses apply to you? _____
_____
_____

FRIDAY

Ready or Not, Here I Come!

David's mouth dropped. "Better prepared? How did I know you were coming? You never sent me a note. You never called me on the phone. I'm only seventeen. My parents never told me about this."

Death replied, "Every time you went to a funeral, every time you passed a graveyard, every time you had a brush with disaster, I reminded you. In fact, as you have gone through high school, my reminders have come almost daily. But as usual, you listened a moment and said, 'It's a long way off.' Well, I'm sorry, but today is the day. I've done my best. I run an honest service here. Now, I've got to get back to the count. Three . . ."

"But what about the millions who haven't heard? I suppose they get the same treatment, but they haven't even had a chance."

"First," said Death, "the Master always deals with everyone with justice. Second, you have heard. You're responsible for you, not them. Anyway, this is taking a bit longer than I planned. I really have to move on."

David pointed the gun at the shadow. But he realized such a tactic was useless. Suddenly, an idea hit him. "Look, Death, I've heard of people being saved at the last minute, on their deathbeds. Is that really possible?"

Death was quiet a moment. Then he said, "Yes, it's possible. I'm not usually one to say such things, but all things are possible with him. I've seen many deathbed conversions. There's always time to repent and believe as long as you're alive."

104

"Then I could do it right now, right?"

"Of course. Any time so long as you're still alive. I would be very glad to see it." Death waited.

Perfect Harmony

Preachers and theologians have summarized the gospel many different ways. There's the Romans Road, using a number of verses from Romans. There are *The Four Spiritual Laws* and a booklet called, *How to Have a Happy and Meaningful Life.*

These are all sound and helpful methods. But what is the gospel? How could we simplify it to its barest elements? First, God. God is holy, loving, just, all-powerful, all-knowing, and everywhere present. Because he is just and holy, he must punish sin. Because he is loving and gracious, he wants to forgive sin. Because he is righteous, he cannot tolerate any sin at all.

That creates some problems for us, but also for God himself. How can he both forgive sin and punish sin at the same time? If he can't do both, he compromises his own character. If he forgives, he ceases to be just. If he chooses justice, he negates his grace.

That brings us to us. We are the creations of God, made in his image. We began innocent, free, and righteous. But we all chose to disobey God when Adam and Eve disobeyed. That choice has led to every sin that has ever been committed. As sinners, we deserve God's wrath and punishment. How can we escape it?

That leads us to Christ. Jesus is God's son, the incarnation of God, the second person of the Trinity, completely God and man in one person. He left heaven, came to earth in the form of a baby, was born through a virgin named Mary, grew up, lived a perfect life, made disciples of twelve men, then died on a cross on the Friday before Passover. The following Sunday he rose from the dead, and forty days later he ascended into heaven to reign from there and soon to come back to earth to set up his kingdom.

Now the issue: Do you believe these things? Do you accept your sinful state as forgivable and changeable only by Christ's forgiveness and the indwelling of the Holy Spirit? Do you want to know Jesus personally so that you become everlasting friends? And do you want to see others have the same thing?

God wants us to believe in Jesus and to be transformed into new people through him. When we believe and follow him, repent of our sins and seek to live in relationship with him, we begin our "walk" with Christ. The moment we choose to believe and accept him we are saved.

Does that make sense?

That transaction can take place anywhere, anytime, in anyone. If it hasn't happened to you, why not take that step now? Jesus invites us all to follow him with the words found in Matthew 11:28-30, "Come to me, all you who are weary and burdened, and I will give you rest. Take my yoke upon you and learn from me, for I am gentle and humble in heart, and you will find rest for your souls. For my yoke is easy and my burden is light."

Does anything keep you from coming to him and finding that rest he promises?

Fine Tunin'

1. Perhaps you have already taken that step, recently or years ago. Then the Scripture's words to you are found in Romans 12:1-2. Will you offer to him your body and soul as a living sacrifice that will become your perfect and final act of worship?

2. If you do know Jesus personally, why not take a moment and thank him for being a part of your life? Commit yourself anew to him, to learn of him and walk in the yoke that will prove so easy and light all the days of your life.

Last Chance Saloon

David screwed his face through several contortions, but somehow the more he thought about repenting the angrier he became. He found himself thinking, *What right does God have to demand this of me? Why should I repent now? I have a pro career ahead of me. This is preposterous. I've always hated this kind of thing, and I'm not going to indulge in such nonsense now.*

He turned again to Death. "Death, I need more time to think. I haven't had enough time. Come back tomorrow."

"I'm sorry," said Death. "As I understand it, each person has precisely the time they need. If they don't do it by then, they never do it. So please allow me to do my duty. One . . ."

David fell to his knees. "Please, Death, I will repent. Just give me one more hour."

The shadow moved quickly and enveloped David. David fired the gun. Death quietly said, "Zero," and as David slumped to the floor, Death glanced at David's watch and nodded.

Once again he had performed his service on the dot.

The next day the story took up a minute in the local nightly news. It was mentioned that David batted .414 that season and was certainly on his way to the majors. The commentator also mused about the strange gunshot. But the investigators had come up with no clues as to whether an intruder had come into the office. An autopsy was being performed and the cause of death appeared to be heart failure—very strange in so young a person. The anchorman showed some clips of David batting and fielding. Then, turning to the weatherman, he remarked, "It's a real shame, but I guess death spares no one—not even an MVP."

"Righto," said the weatherman, turning to the camera. "And this may turn out to be a most valuable playing weekend, folks, 'cause we've got a doozy for you."

Perfect Harmony

Perhaps you have read this far and remain skeptical. A youth pastor gave you this book, or a parent asked you to read it. You're still not convinced. Perhaps a letter from a famous Christian author named Dorothy Sayers will help. She wrote many murder mysteries during the 1920s and 1930s about the exploits of Lord Peter Wimsey and another character named Montague Egg. In her later years she turned to theological plays and essays. On one occasion a scientist asked her to write a letter to his scientific organization about why she believed in God and Christianity. Her reply opened with a string of questions:

> Why do you want a letter from me? Why don't you take the trouble to find out for yourselves what Christianity is? You take time to learn technical terms about electricity. Why don't you do as much for theology? Why do you never read the great writings on the subject, but take your information from the secular 'experts' who have picked it up as accurately as you? Why don't you learn the facts in this field as honestly as in your own field? Why do you accept mildewed old heresies as the language of the church, when any handbook of church history

will tell you where they came from?

Why do you balk at the doctrine of the Trinity—God the Three in One—yet meekly acquiesce when Einstein tells you $E = mc^2$?

I admit, you can practice Christianity without knowing much theology, just as you can drive a car without knowing much about internal combustion. But when something breaks down in the car, you go humbly to the man who understands the works; whereas, if something goes wrong with religion, you merely throw the works away and tell the theologian he is a liar.

Why do you want a letter from me telling you about God? You will never bother to check on it or find out whether I'm giving you personal opinions or Christian doctrines. Don't bother with me. Go away and do some work and let me get on with mine.[8]

Before you head off to do something, what is *your* answer?

Fine Tunin'

1. If you're still unconvinced, read the story of Thomas and Jesus in John 20:24-29. What do Thomas's statement and Jesus' reaction indicate about how God feels about our doubts, questions of fact, and desire to know the truth?

2. A primary excuse people use for not believing in Christ is this: "I heard the Bible is full of contradictions and you just can't be sure it's true." Well then, why not follow Dorothy Sayers' counsel and find out for yourself? Begin reading the Gospel of Mark and finish it. In the

process, ask God to show you the truth. You may be surprised how he will work in your heart.

Notes

1. This story adapted from Mark Littleton, "The Count," *Tales of the Neverending* (Chicago, Ill.: Moody Press, 1990), 185-190.

2. John Myers, *Voices from the Edge of Eternity* (Old Tappan, N.J.: Fleming H. Revell, 1968), 33.

3. Ibid., 46-48.

4. Ibid., 61.

5. Ibid., 48.

6. Ibid., 45.

7. Ibid., 34.

8. Dorothy Sayers, Quoted in *Christianity Today*, 11 December 1981, Vol. 25, No. 21, 13.

WEEK FIVE

Marching to the Beat of a Different Drummer

PEOPLE TOLD HIM IT COULDN'T BE DONE.
NO ONE COULD PLAY THE PIANO IN A
MARCHING BAND. BUT CHUCK DIDN'T LISTEN TO THEM.

MONDAY

Fox of the Year

Ken Willis pulled open his locker and looked over the stack of books in the top sections. He placed his history books in the bottom and took out the English text for his next class. As he thought about the test he had the next period, he suddenly became aware of fingers tickling his back. A moment later, his girlfriend, Lisa Summers, slid up behind him and covered his eyes with her hands. "Guess who?" she whispered huskily into his ear.

Instantly, he felt turned on, thinking to himself, *She's got to be the prettiest girl in school.*

"Just thought I'd give you a little romantic sendoff to your *Romeo and Juliet* test," she said huskily.

Ken pressed her into the locker and kissed her on the lips, then drew back and glanced in both directions down the hall. "If one of the monitors sees us, we're dead meat," he whispered.

"Let them do their worst." Lisa kissed him again, then wriggled free. "I hope that gets you in the mood."

Ken rolled his eyes as the bell rang. "See you in Algebra."

She blew him a kiss and hurried down the hall. He watched her dress swish sexily and then told himself to calm down. "Lord, I can't stand it," he said. But he forced himself into test mode and hurried off to the English class.

After the test Todd James caught Ken going up the stairs to their social studies class. They were good friends, though Todd had none of the Christian beliefs Ken held. "You and Lisa are getting pretty tight, my man."

"Yeah," Ken said with a grin. "I'm in love."

Todd laughed. "So, you gettin' any?"

Ken's eyes narrowed. "What do you mean by that, Todd?"

"You know what I mean."

Ken stiffened. He hated this kind of banter even though he was used to it. Todd and he were in a rap band that Ken played lead guitar in, and he and Lisa had double-dated with him and his girlfriend, Sarah, several times. Still, Todd talked too much about sex and often made Ken angry. Ken had witnessed to him several times and even invited him to the small community church he and Lisa attended. But Todd said he wasn't ready for religion.

Ken answered, "We don't do that kind of stuff."

Todd snorted. "Yeah, right, boss man. You're just keepin' the good stuff to yourself. You know 'bout Lisa's sister and my brother, Ray, don't you?"

Ken felt his face become hot. "Lisa and I aren't that way."

Ray had gotten Lisa's sister, Carolyn, pregnant two years before. She and her baby were living at home now and Ray had disappeared, supposedly to work on the streets.

"Get off it. I know she's just like her sister. And Ray told me plenty about her."

Ken pushed past Todd to the stairwell. "Lisa is a good girl and we have certain beliefs, man. I don't want to hear any more about this. Understand?"

Todd grinned as he stuck next to Ken up the stairs. "Yeah, well then you best cool her off. She knows how to turn a guy on."

Ken knew that was right. But where did you draw the line? Couldn't you have a little fun without compromising basic beliefs?"

Perfect Harmony

Learning to show affection, developing warmth and style, even being sexy, are all part of being human. In our teen years we first begin to experiment with heterosexual relationships. We want to know what it's all about. We long to feel those beautiful emotions, those deep, piercing joys of being in love and close and one. There are few things more wonderful in life than genuine affection and love for another person. There are few things more disappointing than being used or giving more than you've got or throwing away what is precious on a whim.

That is why sex is so fabulous and so dangerous. It's an offering of the whole self. For that reason it should be given—at any level—only in the right context. The Scriptures command us to experience certain things only in marriage, where a legal, public, and social commitment has been made. Those things we know well: sexual intercourse and certain elements of the process that leads up to it. To compromise on these truths invites certain disaster. Maybe not immediately. Maybe not for many years. But no one can compromise his or her purity before God without consequences.

Consider two scriptures. First, the seventh commandment: "Thou shalt not commit adultery." Jesus made the truth clear in Matthew 5:27-28: "You have heard that it was said, 'Do not commit adultery.' But I tell you that anyone who looks at a woman lustfully has already committed adultery with her in his heart."

"Looks at lustfully." That covers a lot of territory. The principle is that any form of sexual relations outside the bond of marriage is adultery in God's eyes.

There's also Proverbs 5:15-17: "Drink water from your own cistern, running water from your own well. Should

117

your springs overflow in the streets, your streams of water in the public squares? Let them be yours alone, never to be shared with strangers." In the context, Solomon refers to sex.

Waiting for the time when you have your own "cistern," though, can be agonizing and difficult. What makes it worse is the pressure put on us by our friends, like Todd. How do we handle both the internal pressure of wanting to have sex and the outward pressure of society which so often makes virginity and purity the conviction of fools?

That is the issue we will explore in this chapter.

Fine Tunin'

1. Read Jesus' words in Matthew 5:27-28. Why do you think God considers lust as the equivalent of adultery? What is God warning us about? Why does he take such a strong stand on the issue? _____

_____

2. How can a young person begin to control his lust and still experience some of the joys of heterosexual relationships? How far can we go? How necessary is it to have strong convictions before we ever begin the process?

_____

_____

_____

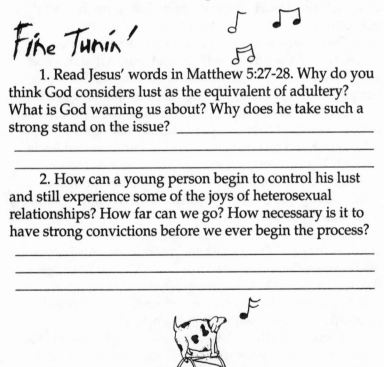

TUESDAY

Party Time

That weekend Ken and Lisa went to a party where the band was playing. She hung around at the fringes, talking to friends and watching the band play. On breaks they sat down and cuddled a little. But Lisa, though she could be sexy, didn't like letting it all hang out as some girls did. She put her head on Ken's shoulder and they whispered quietly, just enjoying one another's warmth.

When Ken went back for the band's next set, Todd snickered. "Gonna get some after the party tonight, Ken?"

Ken gave him a hard look, but said nothing. Then the band began playing some rather lurid material that Ken had tried to get them all to stop. It was too late. Afterward Ken apologized to Lisa.

When Todd walked over to them, joking and acting up, Lisa gave Todd a sour look and didn't join in the banter. After he drifted away, she said, "I don't like you hanging around with him."

Ken shrugged. "Todd's all right." But he knew precisely what she was referring to. Several months before she'd unloaded some of her anger about Todd's brother pressing Carolyn to have sex with him until she finally gave in to please him. Lisa swore she'd never go out with someone like that.

Ken knew he had to talk about some of the things Todd insinuated, but he didn't know how to broach the subject. Everything he thought to say sounded wrong. Finally, he gave her a quick kiss. "Let's just have a good time. And let's pray for Todd. He just needs to become a Christian."

"He needs more than that."
"What?"
"A good kick."
Ken laughed and wrestled her closer on the couch.
Lisa wriggled away. "Coming back to life, I see."

Perfect Harmony

In a typical high school there are tangles of relationships all over the landscape. Older brothers and sisters have blazed a trail that the younger siblings will follow. Occasionally, as in Lisa's case, an older sister or brother will have made mistakes that leave the younger ones in one of two situations: either they decide they will never repeat such behavior, or they fail to reckon with the consequences and end up making the same errors.

Lisa and Ken are obviously experiencing the first pangs of real love. Certainly their biological desires move them to want to go all the way. But they both also have convictions about the issue because of their Christian commitments.

The bigger problem in the equation is Todd. He goads and taunts Ken, making him feel a little less than a man because he has not "done the deed" with Lisa. It's a typical pressure brought to bear on all young people sooner or later. How do you deal with it?

First, you can fight it. But a lot of people might end up laughing at you all the more. They think you're not only foolish, but prudish. They might even accuse you of being gay or lesbian.

Second, you can lie about it. You can make up stories just to get people off your back. "Oh, I'm not a virgin. I've done it lots of times." "Me? Get out of here! I lost my virginity last summer with . . ."

Third, you can ignore it. But that does little good. Your own hormones echo the thoughts of your taunters. You know very well you'd like to make it with somebody. The only thing that prevents you is lack of opportunity, fear of a disease, parental teaching, or a desire to please God.

For a Christian there is still another way. We'll look at that later.

Before we do, though, here's a quote from C. S. Lewis reminding us of the truth of God's motives about allowing sex only in marriage. "We are half-hearted creatures, fooling around with drink and sex and ambition, when infinite joy is offered us. Like an ignorant child who wants to go on making mud pies in a slum because he cannot imagine what is meant by the offer of a holiday by the sea. We are far too easily pleased."

Fine Tunin'

1. Read Solomon's soliloquy in the Song of Songs 4:1-16. Many Christian couples read this book the first night of their honeymoon. What kind of love is portrayed? Is it the kind of love worth waiting for? _____

_____

2. Name several couples in your church who appear to be happy. Consider asking them to talk to your group about marital love.

WEDNESDAY

Feeling the Power

Later that night as Ken drove Lisa home, she sat next to him in the front of his father's Caprice. He draped his arm over her shoulders and thought about whether to stop at a spot in a local park he'd discovered by a small lake. He wasn't sure how Lisa would react if he took her there.

Trying to be subtle about it, he edged off the main drag to catch the highway out to the lake.

Lisa stabbed him with a finger in his tickle spot on the side. "Where are we going, loverboy?"

"Just thought I'd show you the moon."

Lisa cuddled against him. "I think we really ought to head home. My parents want me in by twelve."

"Oh, it's just a little look at the moon. I'll have you home in time."

"Maybe we should look at it from my back yard."

Instantly, Ken was irritated. "Lisa, we've been going out for several months. I think we ought to get off on a little romance now and then."

"I thought we just did." Her voice flared, higher pitched. He could tell she was nervous. He'd seen her like this before when she was afraid. He pressed her far shoulder with his right hand. "It's okay, Lise. Don't worry. It'll be fun."

She said nothing, but as they neared their destination, she stiffened. "Ken, I just don't think we should go out there. Two girls I know got pregnant last year . . ."

"What—are you some kind of prude?"

The moment he said it, he knew it hurt. She didn't

answer, but sat taut and unyielding in the seat. Before he stopped, Lisa was crying.

He cuddled her again, then kissed her forehead. "I'm sorry. I really am. Come on, let's just take a walk. The cool air'll feel good."

They got out of the car and Ken took her hand. He led her down to the water, then dropped her hand and stooped to pick up a flat stone. He sidearmed it out over the water, skipping it five or six times across the surface. After several throws, he laid his arm over her shoulder and held her close. She kept her arms crossed. They stared out at the water and listened to the night sounds. Then he turned her face to his with his hands. "You know you can trust me, Lisa."

She nodded, looking down, then up into his eyes. The moonlight on her face made her look beautiful and he kissed her deeply, pressing her close. His passion rose and he gently guided her onto the grass. They sank down on it, kissing and caressing one another's backs. A moment later his hand was on her breast.

Instantly, Lisa pushed away. "Ken!" She pushed herself to her feet and stood. "I'm going to the car. I want to go home."

"Lise! It's just a little thing. I didn't . . .

"It's not little to me. You know how I feel and what I feel comfortable with in our relationship—I want to go home." She turned and walked toward the car.

Perfect Harmony

Romance is so beautiful, so spontaneous, so effervescent and natural to a couple who are love, it's hard to be restrained in any situation. Our culture doesn't help. Popular books, movies, and TV shows portray sex as the normal and natural outcome of any warm encounter with anyone. First date. First night out. Where should you end up if you like one another? In bed, of course.

What these shows don't portray are the consequences of such encounters. Our country is now in the midst of several epidemics, not only of AIDS, but also gonorrhea, syphilis, herpes, and numerous new and old diseases we once thought we'd beaten. Teenage pregnancy is higher than it's ever been in American history. Some unwed mothers who actually birth their babies (over 50 percent have abortions) end up at the bottom of the economic heap, on welfare, with no future, no hope, and nothing but regrets.

But portraying the negatives rarely punches the pause button on the sex tape deck. We want what we want when we want it—and don't tell us otherwise. Someone has said, "Sex is like fire. In a fireplace, it's warm and delightful. Outside the fireplace, it's destructive."

While it's important to have healthy attitudes about sex and not to be ashamed or afraid of our sexuality, sex outside of marriage has consequences. Hugh Hefner, founder of *Playboy* magazine and builder of a sexual empire, said, "Sex is a biological necessity. Find yourself a girl who is like-minded and let yourself go. It's no different than eating and drinking."

But who would drink gasoline and then smoke a cigarette? Who would eat a stick of dynamite and then do some fire-eating on the side?

God wants us to experience the beauty of sex. But he says there's only one way: within a God-blessed marriage. If you want real joy and beauty, wait until marriage. If you want short-lived thrills that, like a roller coaster, get you nowhere but dizzy, go for anything you want. The only problem is that life isn't a roller coaster ride lasting two minutes; it's many years of living with the results of your choices.

Fine Tunin'

1. Read some of Solomon's thoughts on friends and the results of being friends with the wrong people: Proverbs 1:10-19; 16:29; 12:26; 24:1-2; 24:19-20. What principles can you apply as a result of what Solomon says?

_____
_____
_____

2. Outline three solid reasons, biblical or otherwise, for waiting to engage in sex until marriage. _____
_____
_____

THURSDAY ♪

A Silent Drive in the Night

The silence on the drive home was brutal. Ken was convinced it was over between them. But when they reached her house, Lisa turned and faced him. She said, "I don't know what's going on. I'm willing to let it go this time. If you don't press me about it, we can keep dating. Otherwise . . ."

Then she was crying and he held her, trying to think of something to say. She sobbed, "Ken, I don't want to lose you. But . . ."

He murmured, "It's okay. Don't worry about it. Maybe that's just not for us. I won't do it again."

They both calmed down, and he took her to the door, giving her a kiss before he left. On the way home, he thought about what had happened and tried to put it all together. He knew certain things were reserved for marriage, at least if he was going to hold to a Christian outlook. He also knew he had to do something to deal with Todd. The pressure Todd put on him was real, and already it had made him do something he regretted.

But he also knew that he wanted to do things with Lisa, more than just kiss. How could he control it? He had no idea, and it worried him. He knew in time he might be able to get Lisa to compromise her convictions. As he drove he prayed, but no answer came into his mind.

On Sunday in church, Lisa sat with him as always. Her parents and family filled the whole pew. Carolyn and her little boy, Jason, sat on the end. Ken's mind wasn't on the sermon, though. Something a teacher said in the youth

126

class struck him. "Lay aside lying and speak truth." It occurred to him that instead of fighting Lisa, maybe he could get her on his side.

After church in the parking lot, he told her everything that Todd had been saying and what he'd been feeling. She remained tense through the whole explanation, but when he was done she was angry. "You need to put Todd in his place. What right does he have to . . . I feel like telling him off myself. There are more kids having babies out of wedlock today than ever. You'd think he'd have some sense." She paced as she talked, fuming. "I'm gonna call him this afternoon and let him have it."

"Lise, let me handle it. Todd's a friend, even if he's making a mistake."

"Some friend."

"Lise, please." Todd touched her hand. "I'll handle Todd, okay?"

"You better."

Perfect Harmony

I said earlier that I would give you a fourth and biblical way of dealing with the pressure of sex. One element of it is revealed in this passage: discuss it. The purpose is not to persuade your beloved to do something wrong. It's simply to get the problems out in the open. Paul said, "Have nothing to do with the fruitless deeds of darkness, but rather expose them. For it is shameful even to mention what the disobedient do in secret. But everything exposed by the light becomes visible, for it is light that makes everything visible" (Ephesians 5:11-14).

Evil's habitation is darkness. It thrives in the dark and feels comfortable only when it can do its ugly deeds without being seen. But turn on the switch, throw open the curtains and suddenly evil isn't so eager to do its dirt.

One of the Christian's best and most often forgotten weapons is openness, honesty, forthrightness, and integrity. Turn on the light. Tell the truth. Make it plain. Evil will suddenly shrink in power before the onslaught of the light.

How many movies have you seen recently where the evil deeds were done in darkness or out of sight? Almost all of them. Evil sticks to the back streets.

Ken's decision to tell Lisa what was going on was a wise one. Not only could she understand and sympathize with what he was feeling, but she could also begin to help him. Two are always better than one. Hiding things from her only made the situation worse. But bringing it out into the open enabled them both to find a way through and out.

Granted, these are two kids committed to the truth. But if they weren't, neither should have been hanging out with the other. No Christian has any business being intimate friends with unbelievers who can lead them astray.

Nonetheless, by telling her the truth, Ken defused the power of evil. Now Lisa could get into the battle with him.

Fine Tunin'

1. Read Ephesians 4:25-27. What principles are enclosed in this passage? How do they relate to Ken and Lisa's situation?

2. How often do you find yourself fudging the truth to hide evil? What can you do to bring real honesty and integrity into your relationships? What principles might you apply?

FRIDAY

Facing It

On Monday morning Todd stood at Ken's locker, waiting. Ken hadn't seen Lisa. He wanted to deal with Todd before she showed up. As Ken whirred the reel on the combination lock, Todd said, "Well, is she still a virgin?"

Ken kept his eyes on the lock, patiently moving to the correct numbers.

Todd said, "Come on, Mr. Sex Machine. Did she put out or not?"

Ken turned to Todd and said evenly, "Look, man, I'm not into that scene. Neither is Lisa. I don't want to hear anymore about it. You got it?"

Todd stepped back. "Whoa, who died and made you the big boss?"

Ken made a move toward Todd, thought better of it, and said coldly, "Look, I'm serious. Lay off. I said I'm not into that stuff. If I hear any more about this, my next statement is going between your eyes."

Several students stood around gaping, and when Ken noticed them, he let go of Todd, then bent down to look into his locker. When Ken rose, Todd said, "Hey, you want to hang around with Miss Virgin U.S.A., be my . . ."

"There they are!" A girl's voice cut Todd's statement. Both boys looked up. Lisa and two friends including Todd's girlfriend, Sarah, walked up to them. Lisa was obviously angry.

Ken wanted to avoid a further confrontation, but Lisa started talking before he could say anything. She took a firm stand in front of him. "Just who do you think you are, Todd?"

129

Todd shifted his feet, but obviously wasn't going to give any ground. "What're you talking about, Lisa?"

Ken stepped between them. "Lise, let me . . ."

Lisa moved around him. "You got a big mouth, Todd. Real big."

Todd glared at Ken. "What have you been telling her?"

Lisa said, "You can talk to me, Todd. I'm standing here."

Todd's lips curled into a snarl. "You little whore. What lies have you been telling him? We know what your family's like. Your beauty queen sister. We know what she does and does real well. What's the difference between you and her? You think you're all . . ."

Ken's fist caught Todd dead on the jaw. He fell back against the locker, his lips bleeding. Ken was about to throw another punch when he noticed Lisa was crying and a teacher was stalking down the hall toward them. His ears seemed to be filled with a loud rushing noise like the sound of the open end of a large conch shell.

Perfect Harmony

Things rarely turn out the way we expect. I had hoped to give this story a happy ending. But reality doesn't always offer happy conclusions. Standing up for what's right doesn't guarantee things will work out as we hoped.

Todd's attitude, though, is quite real. Often when confronted about sin, the sinner reacts with anger, possibly violence. In this case, it was Ken who finally reacted to Todd's mean words. Do you think Ken was out of line? What do you think he might have done otherwise?

One action would have been cutting himself off from Todd completely. But he should have done that earlier. Or at least made it clear that their friendship was riding on Todd's willingness to lay off his sexual taunts.

Another might have been a confrontation without Lisa present. Ken should have taken Todd to a neutral place and "read him the riot act," as a relative of mine says. That is, he should have confronted Todd in a place where little could happen except between Ken and Todd. Unfortunately, Todd tended to show up at the worst moment. That's the way life often is.

A third course of action could have been Lisa and Ken sitting down with Todd, calmly explaining their position and asking him quietly to stop what he was doing.

However, human beings are rarely so reasonable and controlled. This was a highly-charged issue, made worse by the problem relating to Lisa's sister and Todd's brother. Few people can approach such things with quiet candor and humor.

Clearly, at this point in the story things are about as low as they can go. But remember an important truth from Romans 8:28: "We know that in all things God works for the good of those who love him." God could turn even this situation into good. Somehow.

Fine Tunin'

1. What would you have done in Ken's situation? How would you have responded to Todd's words? _____
_____
_____

2. It's easy to call the shots after the fact. But try reading Ephesians 5:11-14 and come up with some creative ideas Ken might have employed in the situation. _____
_____
_____

A Candle in the Darkness

Mr. Johnson, the principal, managed to get everyone calmed down, but Lisa cried softly on Ken's shoulder, murmuring, "He didn't have to say that. He didn't."

Todd seemed more determined than ever not to give an inch. Ken felt caught in the middle, between a friend and a girlfriend and a world with too many broken promises and principles.

Mr. Johnson was over six-foot-six and had once tried out for a pro basketball team. He was usually fair—he had a reputation as one who heard all sides before making a decision. He gently asked what this was all about and Ken began to explain, but as the words slipped out they suddenly sounded foolish and strange.

Mr. Johnson turned to Todd. "Do you have anything to add to this?"

"He didn't have to go smacking me in the teeth."

Ken hung his head slightly, but when he noticed Lisa's makeup was streaked and how small and vulnerable she looked, he felt the anger returning. "Don't you know we have a big problem around here? Kids having babies and not taking care of them. Not even getting a high school diploma. Ending up on the street with nothing. Lisa and I don't want that. What's wrong with you?"

Todd clenched his fist and started to stand, but then seemed to reconsider.

Lisa choked, "You don't know what it's like, Todd. My sister Carolyn—it's over for her. My parents have to show her how to take care of Jason. She's a teenager and now she's hanging out with another irresponsible moron. I don't want that. That's all. You don't have to apologize, but I wish you'd just lay off Ken. That's all. We're under enough pressure without that."

Todd looked from Lisa to Mr. Johnson. A nurse brought in an ice pack for his cheek. He held it up to his lips.

Ken said, "I'm sorry about the shot. I just lost it." He held out his hand. "I don't want to see Lisa hurt."

Todd's eyes flickered and he glanced at Mr. Johnson, then at Ken, finally at Lisa. He said, "I'm sorry, Lisa. Guess it's just the way things are. I'm sorry about Carolyn, too. My brother was a loser. She just should have realized that."

Lisa murmured, "We just want to be loved, Todd. With real love. Not gimme love."

Todd looked at the floor. You could tell he was listening, but he wouldn't say anything.

They filed out of Mr. Johnson's office. As they stepped out into the hall, Mr. Johnson said, "Come to the gym this afternoon at four. I'll show you a good way to calm those hormones."

"How?" Ken asked, surprised.

"Hoops, man." Mr. Johnson grinned and Todd, Ken, and Lisa laughed. "We'll be there," Ken said.

"I'll be there, too," Lisa added and they headed down the hall.

Perfect Harmony

Certainly there was no easy way to settle this problem. Peer pressure over sex is one of the toughest issues all of us face from high school until marriage. For many, it's a race to lose your virginity. First one to do it is the winner.

That's the way of the world. Satan will do anything to

destroy God's world. Sex is one of God's best gifts and therefore something Satan longs to corrupt.

We need to remember one thing. Todd was not—could not—come at this issue from a Christian point of view. It was up to Ken and Lisa to try to communicate that perspective to him, even though he might never understand. Christians make a grave mistake when we think others will automatically comprehend and accept our outlook. It rarely works that way. They'll ridicule it. They'll reject it. They'll rip it to pieces logically. But they won't treat it with real respect unless they choose to become Christians themselves.

In this story God somehow did work it for good. Lisa and Ken's convictions came out. Todd realized he'd hurt them both.

Remember the words of Jesus: "With man this is impossible, but not with God; all things are possible with God" (Mark 10:27). He spoke those words in reference to salvation, but they certainly resound with a truth about life itself. God is able to work around our mistakes and somehow transform debacles and disasters into major defeats for the devil.

And what about real sex? Charlie Shedd speaks of how one woman described the beauty of God-gifted sex in his book, *Letters to Karen*: "I had always thought that sex begins at breakfast. A few tender words to start things off would mean so much. Then perhaps a phone call sometime during the day. Some endearments exchanged when he comes home and maybe some help with the supper dishes. Talking things over after the children are in bed. Exchanging ideas. Discussing what we've been doing during the day. A love pat here and a few kisses at the right time. . . . I thought sex could begin at breakfast, build up during the day, and then explode in bed at night."[1]

If any truth can be gleaned from that, it's this: sexual

relations are the outcome of a relationship that lasts all day, all week, all year. In other words, marriage. Anything less is a cheat, a rip-off.

Fine Tunin'

1. Once again, read Solomon's words in the Song of Songs 7:1-13. How can you begin now to prepare yourself for that kind of relationship in marriage? _____

_____

_____

2. Write down a list of three biblical principles you want to hold to about sex until marriage. Put them in your wallet or purse. Pray over them and refer to them frequently. Only personal conviction can help you hold to the principles that will lead to life.

Note
1. Charlie Shedd, *Letters to Karen* (Nashville, Tenn.: Abingdon Press, 1977), 100-101.

WEEK SIX

Tooting Your Tuba

HOPEFULLY THE RECRUITING DRIVE WOULD HELP TO BRING IN SOME NEW MEMBERS. IN THE MEANTIME, THE BAND MEMBERS DID THE BEST THEY COULD.

MONDAY

New Guy in School

John Compaine surveyed the lunchroom briefly. Being new in the neighborhood, having just moved to Pennsauken, New Jersey, from Albany, New York, was tough enough. But the first week of school always scared him. He hadn't been great at making friends, even in Albany where he'd lived for seven years. In a way he just hoped he'd make decent grades this year. The best he'd done last year was Bs and Cs.

He spotted a long table toward the north end of the cafeteria where a group of guys sat, some with bag lunches, others with trays of the daily fare. John swung his bag lunch to get an idea of the contents. His mom never let him buy. "I want to make sure what you have is nourishing," she always said.

He walked cautiously toward the table, trying to size up the row of guys sitting down. An empty chair sat at one end, with a lone longhair munching Cheetos in the last seat. He thought he'd seen the guy in English class. "Anyone sitting here?" he asked hesitantly.

"Take it," the longhair said with a quick smile. "No one around here has reserved seats."

John sat down. The guy had black hair, combed across his forehead, sharp blue eyes, and a chiseled face. "You're in my English class," John said.

"Yeah," he answered. He held out his hand. "Hal Patterson. What's your name?"

John told him, shook hands, then opened his bag. He spied the roast beef sandwich, an apple, and some sliced carrots.

"Watch out for that Rossovich," Hal said. "He's tough. No curve. You better get down Shakespeare. The guy thinks Shakespeare created the heavens and the earth."

John laughed. "Sounds like you've been around."

"Lived here all my life. Where're you from?"

"Albany—for a few years. Before that, Ohio."

John noticed Hal wore a gold necklace with a cross dangling at the end. They talked about sports and some events in the news. When Hal finished his lunch, another guy came by and caught Hal's attention. Hal stood, crumpling up his bag. "Good meeting you, John. See you in English."

John nodded.

As Hal moved away from the table, he heard the other guy mention a rock concert to Hal. John heard the stranger say, "The youth group has over thirty unbelievers coming."

Hal responded, "Yeah, well let's not overpower them."

John froze a moment. Hal wasn't some religious fanatic, was he?

Perfect Harmony

Have you ever wondered how unbelievers look at us believers? While most of us are a bit afraid of witnessing, causing a scene, starting a ruckus, or forcing a confrontation, it's also true that those who don't know Christ may be just as afraid of the encounter as we are. Many people today regard the average Christian as a fanatic just this side of full psychosis. They don't understand why we believe what we believe and they suspect we're hypocrites, at the very least, who think we're better than everyone else.

Actually, Christians of all people should have true

humility. We know if we have anything going it's because of God. We know that we have nothing to boast about except that Jesus opened our eyes. We have no reason to put ourselves above others, or even below. Really, a Christian should be just "one of the guys" or "girls" as the case may be—with this variation: we seek to obey the Lord's Word. That's what sets us apart.

What, then, does the Bible say about witnessing? As a beginning point, try Colossians 4:5-6: "Be wise in the way you act toward outsiders; make the most of every opportunity. Let your conversation be always full of grace, seasoned with salt, so that you may know how to answer everyone."

"Make the most of every opportunity." Let your words be "full of grace." Season them "with salt." Brave, high, powerful words.

Fine Tunin'

1. Think of several opportunities you may have had today to say something to someone about Jesus. How did you approach it? What words did you use? What was the person's response? _____

_____

_____

2. Look at Jesus in John 4:4-26 with the woman at the well. How did he season his words? How did he speak so that the woman listened? _____

_____

_____

TUESDAY

Big Issue on a Little Campus

All that week, if Hal spotted John sitting alone, he came by and invited himself into the next seat. John soon learned Hal was a solid A student who wanted to go to Yale and be an engineer.

Then one Wednesday Hal invited John to his youth group, Breakaway. "We usually just have a lot of fun," Hal said. "I'll warn you, though, someone always gives a short talk from the Bible. But it's no pressure or anything."

John said, "I'm Jewish."

Hal shrugged. "I thought you might be. But that's okay. There're a lot of kids who come from all different backgrounds."

"I'll think about it."

Hal smiled. "Don't sweat it. No pressure, okay? It's just fun. We went to a concert a couple weeks ago and we're going to an Eagles game after Thanksgiving. If you want to come, you're invited."

John grimaced. "Yeah, well, I've got to get to my locker." He had hoped to find some other Jewish guys at the school, but it appeared to be more of a blue-collar neighborhood than where he'd lived in Albany.

Then one day at lunch, Hal said, "You know, you're the first Jewish guy I've ever gotten to know."

Instantly, John became wary. He knew plenty about prejudice. Many in his family had warned him, but he decided to hear what Hal had to say. Hal went on, "A lot of people in this town are bigoted about Jews, if you know what I mean."

John said nothing, biting quickly into his roast beef sandwich.

"It's funny," Hal went on, rubbing an eye. "It's easy to be bigoted until you meet someone from the group you're bigoted against."

John coughed and looked up. "What do you mean?"

"Oh, I have an uncle. He says Jews control the world, the financial markets. All that stuff. I love my uncle, but sometimes he's a jerk. I know a kid here in school who thinks Hitler should have been left alone to finish the job."

John's forehead heated up. He clenched his fists under the table. "What are you saying, Hal?"

Hal looked into John's eyes. "What I'm saying is I think it's wrong. But I'd probably be bigoted myself if not for something that happened to me."

"What's that?" John still felt angry, but now he was intrigued.

"Becoming a Christian."

Perfect Harmony

Speaking words "seasoned with salt" means in one sense to whet a person's appetite for more. When we sprinkle salt on a steak, a mound of peas, or even a bit of cantaloupe (as my grandmother used to do! Yuck!), we're not only seeking to bring out the flavor but to whet our desire for more. Salt makes things richer, more savory and delectable. Without, it much of what we eat would be bland and uninviting.

Salt was so valuable in the Roman world that Roman soldiers were often paid in salt. In fact, you may have heard the expression, "he's not worth his salt." It came from a time when salt was the equivalent of money. Commanders paid the foot soldiers salt because it was so valued.

God longs that we learn to speak in a friendly way that invites the listener to want to hear more. How did Hal do? I don't think he figured out what would entice John. But at the same time, as the conversation flowed, Hal saw an opening and he took it. John was curious to know more.

Solomon put it this way: "A word aptly spoken is like apples of gold in settings of silver" (Proverbs 25:11). How powerful a good word can be! A simple expression of encouragement, love, confidence, or insight can click with anyone. We're all looking for something to get us through the day.

Fine Tunin'

1. Before you go on to the next installment, think of what Hal might be about to say. How do you think someone like John might feel discussing prejudice with a Christian? Remember that many Jewish people believe that Christianity has been a greater cause of their misery than anything else on earth. _____

_____

_____

2. Read Proverbs 18:21. What does this passage say about the power of the tongue to help and hurt, to build up and to break down? How can you apply its truth to the things you say to others? _____

_____

_____

WEDNESDAY

 Breaking the Mold

Instantly John steeled himself for some religious talk, but Hal gave him a crinkly smile. "I guess that'll put you off, plenty. But even though I went to church all my life, I wasn't a real Christian until last year. It changed everything."

John squinted at Hal, trying to control his feelings. The roast beef sandwich felt like sand in his mouth. He said a bit sarcastically, "Most Jews think Jesus is the cause of most of their problems."

Hal nodded. "I know. A lot of others think that, too. Jesus caused the Crusades, the Inquisition. Hitler's Germany was largely Catholic and Lutheran and plenty of those people turned on the gas. It's all part of the strategy."

"Strategy?"

"To compromise the real teachings of Christ. I guess you'll think this is crazy, but do you believe there's a devil?"

For the first time John loosened up. Hal was strange, but at least he was honest. "Devil?"

"Well, if you look at it from the perspective of the Bible, then there's a devil—Satan—who's fighting God. Naturally, if the devil wants to destroy the truth, he has to discredit anyone who speaks it. So if Jesus spoke the truth to people, then the first thing the devil has to do is make Jesus look ridiculous or deceiving. And that's precisely what we see in the world."

John knew Hal was a real intellectual. But this broke the mold. How could Hal believe in the devil?

145

Hal went on, "Yeah, if I was the devil, first thing I'd do is make Christians look bad. That's the perfect way to get others to reject the truth."

John was about to speak, but the bell rang. Hal popped his lunch bag, then gathered up the debris from lunch. As he and John stood, he said to John, "If I get overbearing, John, just say so. I know this probably blows you out of the water a little."

John stared at Hal, then laughed. "Okay, I'll admit it. It is interesting. But remember, it's pretty tough for Christians to convince Jews of anything."

Hal smiled. "I'll believe that one."

Perfect Harmony

There's a story about a rather eccentric barber who loved to witness to his patrons. However, he was not always sensitive to the circumstances in which he was witnessing. On one occasion he lathered up a man for a shave, then picked up his razor, poised it at the man's throat, and said, "Sir, are you prepared to meet your God?" Needless to say, the man wriggled out of the seat and fled with the lather still on his face!

Hal tries to be sensitive to John's feelings even as they discuss a prickly and touchy subject. Yet, one of the best ways for a Christian to witness is to open those tough issues and talk about them honestly and forthrightly. Integrity is the name of the game in sharing your faith. Any sign of phoniness or pretense will immediately turn off a listener. But if you demonstrate sure-footed sincerity and unflinching directness, people are frequently impressed and willing to hear more.

Solomon had another good word about the tongue in Proverbs 25:15. There he says, "Through patience a ruler

can be persuaded, and a gentle tongue can break a bone."
Solomon isn't suggesting we go around breaking bones
with our tongues. Rather, he means when someone before
us is hard, stiff-necked, and unwilling to budge, a gentle
word can often win their approval and agreement.

Fine Tunin'

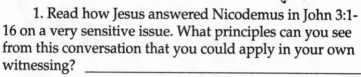

1. Read how Jesus answered Nicodemus in John 3:1-
16 on a very sensitive issue. What principles can you see
from this conversation that you could apply in your own
witnessing? _____

_____

_____

2. Granted, the subject Hal and John are discussing is
sensitive to the point of being explosive. Yet, it's through
speaking honestly about such things that Christians often
win attention and friendship. In a conversation today,
search for an opportunity to show the forthrightness and
integrity of Christ. Then offer an honest word that might
electrify the relationship.

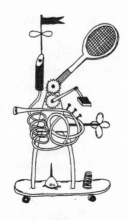

THURSDAY

The Big Event

Shortly before Christmas, Hal told John about a special event his church was sponsoring. "We're learning all about Hanukkah and the lighting of the candles and all that. My pastor asked me if I'd ask you to be a consultant."

John laughed. "You'll do anything to get me to come to your church, won't you?"

Hal shrugged. "Okay, I'll admit it. It's all part of my grand strategy to lead you to Christ. But we do have a local Jewish group coming in to give the talk. And they are all regular Jews—not converted ones. So I thought . . ."

John threw up his hands. "All right. I'll come. I'll make sure they don't make any mistakes. Like I would really know."

Hal clapped him on the back. "Fantastic!"

John rolled his eyes.

"Oh, something else I have on my mind," Hal added. "Would you like to double date sometime?"

John felt his face get hot. "I'm not exactly dating anyone at the moment, Hal."

"That's okay," Hal said. "Neither am I. But I have some friends here and there. I thought you might like to hit a flick or something with some gen-u-ine female companionship."

"You have someone in mind?"

Hal gave him an enigmatic grin. "Maybe."

John picked up his books. "All right, I'll take a chance."

The Hanukkah event went well. The Jewish group from a local synagogue did an excellent job. John didn't notice any mistakes, but he realized he didn't know that much about it. The Breakaway event featured music afterward from a local rock group, then a short talk from an adult. He was interesting, if a bit on the preachy side.

The double date also went well. Hal invited his younger sister, Becky, to be John's date. She was cute, a sophomore with long blond hair, metallic blue eyes like Hal, and an enthusiastic manner. They all talked about basketball at the high school, one of Shakespeare's plays from English class, and about something Hal had read in a science journal about the limits of the universe. John found it all very interesting. Hal had also learned he'd been denied early entrance to Yale. He was disappointed, but everyone encouraged him not to give up.

At the end of the evening, Hal dropped John off and before jumping out of the car, Becky gave him a quick hug. He left feeling mystified and excited, but also a bit worried. During the evening, the youth pastor had read from a psalm of David, Psalm 22. It was an exact description of a crucifixion. He had no idea it was in the Old Testament.

Perfect Harmony

Doing good to others is a primary way we can all witness and open a door that might otherwise be closed. Paul told the Galatians, "Let us not become weary in doing good, for at the proper time we will reap a harvest if we do not give up" (Galatians 6:9).

Notice Paul's emphasis: 1) don't grow weary in doing good, 2) you might feel as if you're not accomplishing much, but 3) God assures us we'll reap a harvest eventually, so 4) don't give up!

It's amazing what a little good can do to a

relationship. A man named Dr. Stuart Holden once spoke of how he met a sergeant of a Scottish Highland regiment who became a Christian through the witness of a godly private. The sergeant spoke of how he and many others in the regiment gave the private a hard time about his faith. One night when everyone was tired and wet, this private came in to bed and knelt down to pray. The sergeant immediately reacted with anger. He kicked the private with soaked and mud-caked boots, then struck him on the side of the head with his hand. The private just went on praying. The next morning the sergeant found his boots clean and shining on the side of his bed. The private had shined them. It broke the sergeant's heart and he became a Christian that day.

Never underestimate the power of both a good word and a good deed. People responded to Christ because he not only said wonderful things but also because he performed great deeds of mercy and love.

Fine Tunin'

1. Memorize Ephesians 4:29, as a good verse about how to speak to others. What clues does the verse give about how we are to talk to others? What steps might you take to get a tongue shaped to this truth? _____

_____

2. Think of a person you may have wronged with cold, unfeeling words. Why not go to them and do some act of good that might win back their heart?

FRIDAY

Help God Open That Heart

After Christmas vacation John asked Hal what had happened about Yale. Hal replied that it didn't look good. "Chances are slim. Everybody's praying about it. But maybe it isn't what God wants. I wouldn't mind going to one of the other places I've applied to, but Yale has been a major dream."

John wondered at Hal's words about "praying about it." Hal was full of such expressions, and yet he was obviously smart. Real smart. It threw John off. Until this year he thought most Christians were dumb. He knew Hal wanted to convert him, as he called it. But one thing Hal had done several times already was ask John what he believed, how Jews looked at life, and what spiritual experiences he'd had. John hadn't said much. In a way there wasn't much to say. But he knew Hal respected him for it and it made him feel good.

At the same time he read some of the passages in the Old Testament Hal pointed out to him. For instance, the place in Psalm 22 about the crucifixion. It troubled him that such an exact description could come from King David, especially when crucifixion didn't even exist. Hal also showed him Isaiah 53, Zechariah 12, and other specific passages that Matthew and Luke quoted as fulfillments of prophecy. It bothered him so much that he talked to his rabbi about it. But the rabbi only said, "There are different ways to interpret all this, John, and I would avoid the young man if he troubles you too much."

To John that wasn't an answer. Just avoid people

because they had good arguments? Just decide you didn't
want to deal with it?

At Breakaway there was a healthy mix of jocks,
studious types, intellectuals, weirdos, and plain fanatics.
But none of them had been offensive. And they all seemed
incredibly committed. He hadn't seen that anywhere else.

It all came down to a very troubling equation. Should
he accept what they believed? Or reject it, even at the peril
of his own understanding of what he read in the Bible?
Could he honestly say Isaiah 53 had nothing to do with
what he knew about Jesus? Could he just overlook other
passages and pretend he didn't know what they meant,
when it appeared so obvious?

Perfect Harmony

John has obviously begun to think about and weigh
the truths he's discovering through Hal's witness. The thing
we need to remember about sharing our faith is that it
involves a relationship. None of us can blithely buttonhole
people, sling them a tract, hit them with a little brimstone,
and expect them to sashay into the kingdom without a
second thought.

Walt Henrichsen tells the story of Dr. H. Clay
Trumbull's encounter with a drinking man on a train. Dr.
Trumbull was a Bible teacher on the way to a speaking
engagement. The man sitting next to him opened a flask
and offered the good doctor a swig of whiskey. Dr.
Trumbull declined. Only minutes later, the man repeated
his offer even more enthusiastically. Dr. Trumbull again
said no. Finally, a third time the man extended the flask to
the Bible scholar. When Dr. Trumbull smiled and said, "No
thank you," the man remarked, "I bet you think I am a
rather evil man doing all this drinking, don't you?"

"No," Dr. Trumbull replied. "I was thinking what a generous man you are to keep offering me a drink."

That word of kindness opened up the doors to a conversation that ultimately led the drinker to Christ before the train trip had ended.[1]

While we should all beware of the temptations to drink, use drugs, and engage in other illicit behaviors, it is important that Christians learn not to reject, condemn, or despise non-Christians for their sinful behavior. When the Pharisees brought a woman caught in adultery to him for his sentence of death, Jesus only replied, "Neither do I condemn you. Go now and leave your life of sin" (John 8:11). Avoiding words of alienation and condemnation help us crack open the hard but broken hearts of those around us.

Moreover, we want people to understand that Christianity is a relationship with Jesus. A growing, dynamic, changing, illuminating friendship with God. It's not just a series of beliefs, following a set of principles, or living by a moral code. It's knowing, walking, talking, and living with someone divine each day of your life. That relationship is what most attracts people to Christ and most to us as Christians. Our goodness may intrigue them. Our arguments may prove them wrong. But it's the relationship—the knowledge that we have someone there with us always and ever who is kind, understanding, willing to listen, and guiding our lives—that makes people want to know God.

Fine Tunin'

1. Read how Jesus handled a similar situation in John 8:1-11. What principles do you see here about witnessing and sharing the faith in a positive, life-enhancing way? __

_____

_____

2. Think back over the past week. How many times did you speak condemning words to or about others? What can you do to avoid condemnation and instead, begin to share uplifting, consoling words to those who hurt? _____

_____

_____

Conversation on a Rock ♪

In the spring Hal invited John to a youth group retreat at a local camp. John almost turned him down, but in the end he had nothing better to do, and he figured he could stave off any fanatical attempts to convert him. Becky would be there—and so would numerous other good-looking girls—so he decided to make the trip.

It was an excellent week. There were plenty of games—capture the flag, football, softball—as well as skits, songs, campfires, and just plain fun. The speakers talked fervently about committing your life to Christ and following him. John listened, but he knew he wasn't ready for the decision they seemed to want.

One afternoon he went down by the lake and sat alone on a rock overlooking it. The lake was beautiful, with the sunlight sparkling off it like fireworks. A fresh breeze carried the scent of the fir trees that surrounded the lake. Then Hal suddenly stood there, looking up at him. "Can I join you?"

John was startled, but he nodded and said, "What's up?"

"Just enjoying the rays," Hal said. He climbed up and sat down. "How do you like the camp?"

"Great. It's a lot of fun." John wasn't pretending. For the first time in his life, he realized Christians were people, just like the rest of the world.

Hal played with a little stick in his hand, then threw the stick into the water. They were both silent. Then, before he could stop himself, John said, "Tell me about how you became a Christian, Hal."

Hal related how he'd been into the party scene and done a little drinking. Then he'd been invited to the Breakaway group by his sister. She'd been going for months. There had been a trip to the beach one weekend. "I accepted Christ there one afternoon, right on the beach." Hal looked away. "It wasn't really dramatic. But that's what happened."

"You accepted Christ?"

Hal smiled. "Yeah, kind of like letting him into my house to live, if you can think of it that way. Like he was going to be my best friend from then on."

"What happened then?"

"Well, I began going to Breakaway and things like that. I started to grow and learn. God began changing me."

"How?" John noticed he didn't even feel uncomfortable.

"Oh, little things. Becoming more patient. Caring more about people. Listening." Hal laughed. "Yeah, listening. That's a big one. And being more aware of what I say and do—even wanting to be a better person. But the main thing . . ."

Hal looked off over the lake and his voice had begun to shake a little. He continued, "The main thing, the thing I almost couldn't believe, was that God, the one who made the whole world, who is all powerful and all everything, that God loved *me* and wanted to be *my* friend. Wanted to spend time with *me*. It blew my mind."

Hal turned to look at John, then held his hand up over his eyes. "Maybe that sounds a little mystical, but everyday I thank him for it. I don't always feel like I love him. I don't always feel like he loves me. But he's there. I know he's there. And he'll never leave. It's a tremendous sense of security. I used to be scared about so many things. School. Life. My dad. But knowing Jesus has given me such security." He smiled at John. "Not that I'm perfect or anything, but knowing him is the greatest thing that ever happened to me."

John swallowed at Hal's sincerity. He knew by the way he said it that Hal believed it completely. It was real to him. In a way John wanted to believe, but he wasn't sure how to make it happen. He wasn't sure if he could deal with the changes in his family life.

"What if I don't accept him, Hal? What would you do?"

Hal laughed. "We'd still be friends. That won't change."

"It won't?"

Hal turned to John and looked into his eyes. The sunlight lit his face and shaded his eyes. John almost flinched away, but Hal said, "John, I love you like my brother. Whatever you do, I'll still love you. But in the meantime, we'll just keep being friends. I can't force you to know Christ. But we can always be friends."

John noticed a slight lump in his throat.

Hal stood. "Come on, we'd better get back. If they think I've converted you there'll probably be a fireworks show."

John laughed. "I can believe that one. They're all probably praying for me, right?"

Hal smiled. "You read us like a book."

They both headed up the trail toward camp.

Perfect Harmony

There used to be a phrase a number of years ago about Christians who witnessed just to convert people. They cared little about who they were, what they needed or wanted, or what feelings they might be hiding beneath the surface. They only wanted to tie another "scalp" to their witnessing belt when that person became a Christian. Such people were called "scalp hunters." Like the proverbial Indian who collected those hairy trophies, his only concern was to rack up a list of spiritual conquests.

What I like about Hal in this story is that his mentality is far from that outlook. He didn't regard John as a specimen, a potential convert whom he'd drop the moment he realized there was little hope of his conversion. No, Hal promised he'd stick with John no matter what decision he made.

That's friendship, the kind that wins souls and claims hearts. After all, making a person a trophy in your showcase is meaningless. But making a friend in this world and possibly for eternity has great value. Both of you will grow through the interaction. Even if John didn't convert to Christ for years, God would use the relationship to change both Hal and John in ways neither could gain without each other.

George Mueller, a founder of orphanages and a multitude of other good works in Britain during the nineteenth century, raised over six million dollars through simple petition to God. He is regarded by many today as one of Christendom's greatest men of prayer. He took everything he could to God and asked him repeatedly to save his friends and enemies, to provide for his orphans, and to meet the needs of the works under his care. He never asked anyone but God for that kind of help.

It is said that Mueller prayed for over sixty years for a close friend to come to Christ. Mueller died without ever realizing the man's conversion. But several years after his death, that man did become a Christian and a committed one.

Witnessing is many things: kind words, friendship, talking about the Bible and your life, being an example, being there when a need arises, listening, arguing, talking late into the night. It's rarely a one-time take-it-or-leave-it encounter. Make your witnessing a gift and work of the heart, and God will surely bless—in ways you can't even imagine.

Week Six

Fine Tunin'

1. Read Acts 1:8 about being witnesses. Just thinking about what you know about the Bible's many examples of witness, what elements do you see that are important? How can you become a better witness? What principles can you apply? ______________________________

____

____

2. Sit down with several Christian friends and come up with a list of people you'd like to befriend, both with the purpose of just being friends and also of sharing your faith. Why not begin praying that God will open up opportunities for you to cross paths and eventually share the truth?

Note

1. Walter A. Henrichsen, *Disciples Are Made, Not Born* (Wheaton, Ill.: Victor Books, 1974), 56-57.

WEEK SEVEN

Drummin' It Out

THIS WAS THE THIRD TIME IN A WEEK THAT
THE STRING SECTION HAD GOTTEN INTO A
DISPUTE WITH THE BRASS SECTION.

MONDAY

What We Have Here Is a Failure to Communicate

Karen Wheeler stared across the table at Linda Bavaro. The yearbook meeting was going as usual, with Karen and Linda disagreeing about everything, from page design to the poetry in the literary section to the arrangement of face photos in the Senior spotlight. They were discussing the layout of the sports slot, and Linda felt strongly that the school's football league champions should be given at least eight pages.

"They won the league championship. They should get a big splash in this year's yearbook," Linda said. "We shouldn't break with Hillsboro tradition anyway."

"It's not tradition!" Karen seethed. Already she sensed that the hot flush that seared onto her face when she became angry was exploding across her cheeks. Linda Bavaro tried to dominate everything she was involved in. "We just don't have to give them everything. You'd think there weren't any other teams represented."

"What are we going to remember twenty years from now—girl's lacrosse?" Linda said, turning to the four others, Jon Holmes, yearbook editor, two other female editors, and the photographer, Grant Hill. "Forget it. People remember football."

"There are numerous other . . ." Karen shot back, as Miss Harris, the yearbook advisor, walked into the office.

"I can hear you two all the way down the hall!" She glared at the two girls. "You'd think there wasn't enough to fight about in the world without two rivals beating each other up about a few pages in a yearbook."

"But Miss Harris, we should be fair," Karen said

limply. "Just because Linda's boyfriend . . ."

"Oh, and I suppose that's what's fair—accusing me of some kind of favoritism or something!" Linda rose and turned to go out. She glared at Jon. "You settle this, Jon. But my vote is cast. And it's not because Cameron is on the stupid football team."

When Linda walked out, Miss Harris looked at Karen, then shook her head. "I've just about had it with you two, Karen. What is this all about?"

Karen sucked her cheek, saying nothing.

Grant shook his head. "We told you they'd never be able to work together."

Miss Harris' eyes narrowed. "I know you told me that, Grant. But . . ." She gazed at Karen. "I thought you two were mature enough to put aside whatever it is that's bugging you and work as a team."

Karen sighed. She looked at her knuckles and said nothing.

It was true. All of it. She and Linda had been best friends a year ago, in the same church and youth group. Then somehow an ugly rumor circulated about Linda getting drunk and supposedly going all the way with a guy named Brian Connett she had just started dating. Karen had an idea how it started—something she'd said to a few friends. But she had never said Linda was drunk, or that she'd had sex with Brian Connett. But she had said . . . Well, what did it matter now? Linda had refused to speak to her again when the youth pastor started asking questions and stories were flying every which way. Karen had tried several times to talk to Linda, but they never even reached the "forbidden subject." Linda simply walked off in a huff each time saying she never wanted Karen "in her face" again.

When Karen didn't answer, Miss Harris sighed. "You two used to be friends—why can't you get along?"

Karen hung her head and looked away.

Miss Harris continued, "If you two don't settle your

differences out of these meetings, I'm going to have you both off the staff. Understand?"

Karen flinched and turned to Miss Harris. "Yes, but I think you'd better tell Linda that, too."

"Believe me, I will."

Perfect Harmony

Strangely enough, often the people who have the greatest difficulty getting along are Christians. Aside from theological issues which separate whole denominations, there are the more simple and yet often paralyzing problems of relationships going sour. One Christian does something to another, there's a confrontation or a nasty rumor, and suddenly friends are parted—sometimes forever.

In American history Thomas Jefferson, vice president of the United States under John Adams, had an excellent and longstanding relationship with his superior, both as politicians and as friends. Then some problems came between them involving family, political appointments, and words supposedly uttered in private. For nearly fourteen years these two famous men split, never talking or writing on friendly terms. Fortunately, their breech was healed by a concerned friend who brought the two men back together.

But they still lost fourteen years of friendship over the matter.

It happens to everyone, including the most sincere, committed, and "loving" Christians.

Notice that in the story Grant and probably many others knew about the tension. They didn't know what to do to change the situation, but try as Karen and Linda might to cover it up, it was plain to all.

When two people part paths, they often think others don't really notice or understand. They may not understand the reasons. But they see the results. And they feel uneasy around both parties. It's often difficult to be friends with two people who dislike each other.

Second, Karen had made several attempts to talk out the problem with Linda. But nothing worked. Again, that's part of the difficulty of a sin or "misunderstanding," which is likely in this case. If you can't get one side to talk, both sides remain hurt and angry.

There are no easy answers here. One place to start is with the Bible. A good verse to start with is Paul's dictum in Romans 12:18, "So far as it depends on you, be at peace with all men" (NASB).

Notice Paul's words—"So far as it depends on you." That is, sometimes the split can't be patched. But don't let it be that way because you personally haven't tried.

Fine Tunin'

1. Read how David tried to patch up his misunderstanding with King Saul in 1 Samuel 24:1-22. Do you think David's actions were wise or unwise? Why? ___

_____

_____

2. What kinds of issues divide Christians today? Name several of the problems you may know about that Christian friends have disputed about. How would you try to "make peace" in such situations? _____

_____

_____

TUESDAY

A Big Issue – to Me!

Yearbook staff meetings went forward. Karen made an effort not to fight with Linda and chose only those rare important issues that she thought were worth debating. Meanwhile, Linda kept a low profile. Then one Saturday when the staff came in to work on a deadline, things blew up over a spilled Coke. Miss Harris was out of the room. Grant and Jon sat at the far table, and Karen and Linda faced each other over a stack of pictures. The two already had argued over whether to include a cute picture of someone showing off in the senior play when Karen accidentally spilled a Coke and ruined it.

"How stupid can you get?" Linda yelled as the Coke poured across the black and white enlargement and streamed toward the other stack of photos.

Karen shot up out of her seat, pulling the other photos away, and mopping at the stream with a ready towel. "The least you can do is try to . . ."

"You clean up your own messes!"

At that moment, Miss Harris stalked in. "Are you two at it again?"

Linda stopped. Karen turned red. Jon and Grant said nothing.

"I'll ask again. Is this another argument?"

Jon said lamely, "A Coke got spilled."

"*Karen's* Coke," Linda said tersely.

"It was an accident," Karen answered, setting her jaw and still mopping at the puddle on the table.

"It's ruined the photo—the very one she didn't like in

the first place." Linda held the picture out to Miss Harris.
"All right, girls, come with me."

Perfect Harmony

Rivalries form quickly and sharply in a high school and college context. Obviously, many arise from a competitive spirit. The football gridiron, the lacrosse field, the school newspaper, and the short story contest all offer ripe ground for a harvest of healthy differences.

As a young Christian I made a mistake with a close friend. He confided in me about his educational career, including the fact that he'd dropped out of high school and later gotten a GED. He now had a bona fide bachelor's degree from an excellent Christian college and was working toward a master's.

I didn't realize how sensitive this issue was to him. But the next week I mentioned it in passing to another friend. Soon, several people knew about it, and the friend who had confided in me was hopping mad!

Fortunately, as Christians we felt it wise to talk it out and I apologized. But that incident scared me. I suddenly realized how easy it is to destroy a close relationship through a wrong move.

We have to get clear about what is important as Christians. Are unity, fellowship, friendship, and love all important, or will we stand on our pride and refuse to reconcile because we feel we've been hurt beyond repair? There are many more things at stake than a friendship. Like what? How unbelievers look at us Christians when we do have problems. How much we are willing to make amends in obedience to God even at a loss to ourselves. Whether we'll make an issue of something trivial (in many cases) or whether we'll work at getting along even when it hurts!

Sooner or later every friendship suffers a break of some kind. Whether that break becomes a permanent cleavage or a wound that heals and makes one stronger is usually up to us.

Fine Tunin' ♪

1. Read Romans 12:18. What do you think Paul meant by "so far as it depends on you"? What kinds of steps are involved there? How much effort are we called upon to reconcile in a broken relationship? _____

_____

_____

2. What molehills do you think could be easily forgiven and forgotten that you've seen people turn into mountains? Why do you think this happens? _____

_____

_____

WEDNESDAY

Closing In

Miss Harris closed the door behind her in the faculty lounge at the other end of the hall from the yearbook office. "Sit!"

Karen slumped onto one end of a couch underneath a Monet painting, folding her arms. Linda hunched on a red vinyl chair at the far end of a tea table. She sucked a string of hair and crossed her legs, kicking the upper one nervously.

Miss Harris took the seat on the far side of the tea table, between the two girls. "I don't get this. The yearbook staff is a team. We have a lot of work to do to meet our deadlines, and you two are causing everyone a lot of tension. I can't have this. Do you both want to be kicked off the yearbook staff?"

Karen sighed and looked down into her lap. She wanted there to be peace between her and Linda, but she didn't want to grovel either. When she looked up, Miss Harris said, "What can we do about this, girls? Things can't continue this way."

"It's been this way for over a year now," Karen murmured.

Miss Harris was a pretty woman, with thick blond hair pulled into a ponytail. She kept to business usually, but once Karen met her at lunch and they talked quite a bit. Karen had been able to tell Miss Harris some about her faith, although Miss Harris cut her off by saying she had to get back to her classroom.

Now, she was clearly frustrated and angry about the

tension between Karen and Linda. After a few moments of silence, Miss Harris said coldly, "Karen I thought you were very religious, into church and everything—and I've heard that Linda is, too."

Both girls looked up. Karen hadn't wanted to discuss this. But she said, "Yes," and glanced at Linda, who agreed without looking back at Karen.

Miss Harris shook her head. "You Christians are all alike—all talk, no show. I have yet to meet one who practices what she preaches."

Karen stiffened. Linda was sullen. Then Karen said, "Miss Harris, I'm really sorry, I . . ." but Miss Harris broke in. "If there is one thing I learned in Sunday school, it's that people, especially Christians, are supposed to love one another, forgive one another, and share with one another when the other is hurting. I know those concepts are pretty much passé in our world, but I did hope some Christians somewhere must practice it."

Karen gulped. But Miss Harris continued, "So what's the problem?"

She looked from Linda to Karen and back. Linda was obviously uncomfortable. Karen dug her fingernails into her palm. Miss Harris shook her head as she stood to her feet. "I want you two to either settle this, or stow it. Do you understand? If you can't, you're both off the yearbook, even though I know it will be hard to fill both of your positions."

Karen had never seen Miss Harris so angry. But before she had a chance to say anything further, the teacher had turned and walked out of the room, leaving Linda and Karen sitting uncomfortably on the edges of their respective seats.

Perfect Harmony

Strangely enough, both of those girls could have recognized something marvelous happening, even though they both felt miserable. What was it? That maybe God was working!

Obviously the Lord did not want to see their friendship over and them hating one another. Karen had tried to talk to Linda. Linda herself probably felt that Karen had tried to do her in with some nasty gossip. It's understandable that both might feel uncomfortable and even angry around each other.

But God is in charge of all of life. And maybe he had engineered this little "meeting" with Miss Harris because there was no other way to get them to talk.

Remember that no matter how bad your problem may be with another Christian, family member, or friend, God is concerned about it. He wants to help. Jesus said, "Blessed are the peacemakers, for they shall be called the children of God." Psalm 133:1 graphically speaks of the joy of real fellowship between believers: "How good and pleasant it is when brothers [or sisters] live together in unity!"

You might feel your situation is unsolvable. Your enemy will never forgive you. You can never rebuild that broken friendship.

But remember your ace in the hole: God himself. He cares. He knows how to bring us together even when we could never plan it or make it happen ourselves.

Centuries ago John Wesley and George Whitefield were two of the greatest evangelists on earth. But they had towering differences of opinion theologically and personally. They had both once been in the same prayer group and Bible study. But for awhile they broke their friendship.

Nonetheless, in their later years they began to put aside their differences. One time a follower of Wesley who did not know of Wesley's love for Whitefield, asked the great man, "Mr. Wesley, do you think you'll see Mr. Whitefield in heaven?"

Wesley is said to have replied, "No, sir. He'll be so close to God's throne and I so far back, that I won't see but the back of his head!"

Here were two men who differed in many ways and yet found it in their hearts to cultivate a deep and joyous love for each other.

Fine Tunin'

1. Have you ever heard some strong criticism by a friend or relative of Christians or Christian groups? What were the judgments leveled? Were they fair? Why or why not? _____
_____
_____

2. Read James 4:11-12. How might this scripture relate to Karen and Linda's situation? How could they apply it in reconciling their conflict? _____
_____
_____

THURSDAY

More Problems

Linda stood quietly. Karen was afraid to look at her face. Karen said quietly, "I guess we are causing one heckuva problem around here, aren't we?"

Karen looked up. Linda's face looked gray, all the blood drained out. Karen felt heavy and close to tears. This was the last thing she'd expected out of Miss Harris. She didn't speak.

Linda's voice was strained when she spoke again. "I don't know about you, but I feel like a real jerk."

"Yeah."

"What can we do?"

"I don't know." For the first time, Karen looked up hopefully. Maybe the ice was melting.

Linda sat down and gazed at Karen. "What do we do?"

Karen answered, "Linda, about that rumor that got started . . ."

Anger crossed Linda's face, but she said nothing.

"I'm sorry for what I said. I never said you got, well, drunk or that you did anything with Brian like that. But somehow . . ."

Linda gazed at her. "What do you mean, you never said those things?"

Karen shook her head. "No, I really didn't. Linda you have to believe me."

"Then what did you say?"

Karen gulped. "It wasn't very nice. I guess I was jealous of you with Brian. I kind of liked him."

For the first time Linda smiled. "Okay, but what did you say?"

Karen looked down and suddenly she stared to cry. This was more difficult than she'd thought. She didn't look up. "I was wrong, Linda. Really wrong."

Linda put her hand on Karen's. Karen almost flinched, but she let it stay. "I said you had drunk at least two beers . . ."

Linda pulled her hand away. "But I didn't have any."

Tears dripped off the end of Karen's nose. "I guess Brian was the one who had them. But . . ."

"But you thought I was drinking, too?"

Karen nodded. "I'm sorry. I'm really sorry."

"But you didn't say I was drunk?"

Karen nodded. "Thank God, I didn't say that. But then Jeannie Evans and Christine Paulis, well, it just got rolling and . . ."

"Did you say anything about sex?"

Karen steeled herself. This was the biggie. She put her hand on her forehead and sobbed.

Perfect Harmony

When you sin against a fellow believer, it's never easy. Especially if it is real sin and you've been caught— nailed in place. Telling a lie about someone—even just a slight exaggeration—can go a long way.

As a seven-year-old, I once got caught playing with matches. When my father talked to me about it and asked where I'd gotten the matches, I lied. I said that a neighbor friend had bought them for me. To my horror, my father decided to go talk to my friend's father about what had happened. I went to bed in mortal terror. When my dad came back that night, he gave me a severe spanking.

But facing my friend the next day was far worse. I wished the world would stop. I wished I'd die and be buried. I hoped we'd move to a new neighborhood.

Nonetheless, I had to face Tommy. When I did, I found an extremely sympathetic and unconcerned kid. He didn't think it was such a big deal. I apologized and the whole thing was forgotten.

But the fear and anxiety leading up to the meeting were terrible.

You can see Karen's fear in the story. She knew she'd sinned, even though she had not said all the things that were added to the rumor later. But her confession was not easy.

It never is. There may be anger, fear, harsh words all around. But the important thing is that we deal with it. David said that when he kept quiet about his sin, his whole body seemed to wither away. He felt weak and terror-stricken. Only when he finally confessed his sin was he freed from the pain (see Psalm 32:1-11).

Fine Tunin'

1. Are there people in your past or recent history whom you've hurt? What would it take to help you go to them and confess your sin? _____

_____

_____

2. Read James 5:16. What does this verse say about confession in the situation that Linda and Karen were in?

_____

_____

FRIDAY

Talking It Through

Karen's whole body shook. Linda reached into her purse and pulled out a Kleenex. She gently handed it to Karen. "Here. It's okay. I'm not angry."

Karen turned to her. "Linda, I was really catty. I said . . ." She took a deep breath. "I said you were making out with Brian so hot and heavy you probably ended up in bed with him." She swallowed. "It was an awful thing to say. I'm sorry. I'm so sorry."

Linda sat there stunned for a moment.

Karen shook her head and dabbed at her eyes. "I don't know how that started. But I can guess."

"Karen, we were such good friends. Why did you do that?"

"I don't know, Lin. I really don't. I was jealous. And we had that little fight the week before about something. I don't even remember what it was now. Something at church. It was so wrong, I know. I hope I never do it again."

"I hope so, too."

Karen looked up. "Do you hate me?"

Linda sighed. "For a long time I did. I thought you were trying to destroy me for some reason. The fight we had was about something I said to you then. You remember we'd just taken the college boards our junior year."

Karen nodded.

"I'd scored higher and said some smug things about how easy I thought the test was. You felt like I was putting you down and I didn't want to admit it."

Karen blinked. "Yeah, I remember now. Why do we do these things to ourselves?"

Linda looked away. "I'm sorry, Karen." She patted her hand. "Come on, let's go get a Coke at the machine. We can stop by the bathroom and fix your makeup."

Karen stood. Suddenly they hugged and both burst into tears. Linda said, "It's been a long time."

"Yeah."

They walked out of the room. As they closed the door, Miss Harris' heels clicked on the hallway.

Perfect Harmony

Whenever you have a problem with another person, remember four steps that can help to heal the break.

1. *Decide to listen.* Give your friend a fair hearing. Remember, they may be scared, or angry, and you need to give them a chance to air their feelings. You might not like what they say, but few people will remain angry with a friend who has given them an honest ear.

2. *Admit your guilt.* If you were wrong, tell them. There's nothing lost in confessing sin, except a little pride and most of us could do with a whack off of that part of our persona.

3. *Commit yourselves to communicate in the future.* There will be other problems. But two people committed to hearing out one another always have a chance at a lasting, forever friendship. So long as the lines are open, there's the possibility that anything, even the worst sins, can somehow be fixed. It's when we refuse to talk it out that there is no hope.

4. *Pray together.* Nothing heals a relationship better than two people "takin' it to the Lord." His presence fills the room and your hearts and suddenly what seemed so

big and impossible now looks small and trivial.

And one other thing.

I always liked the jazz pianist's answer to one heckler as the former banged out a tune on a rickety piano. The critic called out, "Say, where can a fella hear some live music in this area?" The musician didn't miss a beat: "Just wait till I finish typing this letter—okay?"

Don't forget humor. Lighten up. It's probably not a matter of life and death. So laugh a little.

Fine Tunin'

1. Read Romans 13:8. What does this verse teach that we're to do in all relationships? _____

_____

_____

2. Think of one relationship in your life that isn't on the best of terms at the moment. What can you do to try to heal the wounds? _____

_____

_____

WEEKEND

Finding A Way

Things were rocky over the next few weeks, but Linda honestly forgave Karen. Both girls realized how big the problems caused by gossip could be. They resolved not to let it destroy their friendship again.

They still weren't the best of friends as before. There was a little distance. But Karen especially felt confident that would change with time. She simply had to give Linda a chance to see she was going to be a loyal friend again.

Then one afternoon in the office, they had another difference of opinion. Miss Harris sat back behind them as the staff hashed it out. Karen could feel her steely eyes on both of them, but she spoke up first. "I think we should give one page to each team in the school."

"But that's five pages over," Linda said. "That's a fortune. We don't have the money."

Jon and Grant agreed with Linda, but Karen said, "What if we come up with a way to raise more money?"

"Like how?" Linda asked, bending over the table with her critical, you're-a-real-dope look that Karen had seen a million times.

Karen noticed Miss Harris tensing, but she held her ground. "What if we do something to raise money? Other yearbooks have ads at the end. Maybe we could put in some ads and raise . . ."

"Yeah, and who's going to do that?" Linda said.

Jon looked from Linda to Karen. Then he laughed. "I've just decided who's going to build an ad staff."

Karen and Linda turned to him. "Who?"

"You two!"

Karen felt her heart sink. But then her eyes met Linda's. Linda said, "Okay, we just have to build a staff, right? We don't actually have to sell the ads ourselves?"

"Sure," Jon said. "Just build a sales staff. With Karen."

Linda gazed directly at Karen. At the same moment, Karen sensed her legs were weak. But suddenly she liked the idea. She said quietly, "I'm game if you are."

Linda smiled. "All right. Like old times. Selling Reese's Pieces for the church."

Karen laughed. But out of the corner of her eye she noticed Miss Harris roll her eyes with relief. Karen knew their friendship would take some rebuilding, but in her mind she was confident the problem was over.

After the meeting Linda caught Karen in the hall. "Guess what?" she asked, her eyes alight. She didn't wait for Karen to answer. "I saw Brian Connett again."

"Really?"

"Not drunk. Not with another girl. He didn't even recognize me."

Karen laughed. "So who are you after this week?"

Linda laughed. "I don't know. Some stud." Karen chuckled. But she noticed they were walking down the hall together and suddenly it seemed like old times.

Perfect Harmony

Sometimes you can't see daylight until you get to the end of the tunnel. In Linda and Karen's situation, an interesting possibility came into view once they'd taken down the wall that separated them. They might never have seen it, however, by planning. They only saw it as things happened around them.

Many times a renewed friendship is not something

181

we can make happen; rather, it's something the Lord does in our midst by circumstantial or "coincidental" means. We can never discount in a dispute situation the power of God's help.

Jesus works through people. Undoubtedly not only was he doing some things in Karen and Linda, but also through the yearbook staff and Miss Harris. The Lord employs many means to reach his ends. What if Miss Harris had not made the two girls sit down and talk it out? What if Karen hadn't confessed? What if Linda hadn't been willing to listen? Then maybe their friendship would still be nonexistent today.

Fortunately, God in his wisdom and love interceded.

It's a tough world. No one makes it on his own. Each of us must learn to give, take, speak, listen, put out, and pull in.

If you find yourself in a dispute situation, get some help. Work at making peace and rely on people around you to encourage and offer wisdom. Above all, God wants us to get along. No, more than that: he longs that we *love* one another. That's not accomplished on a feeling. It takes work, effort, determination, and commitment.

But it's possible for those who decide to go for it!

Fine Tunin'

1. Earlier we discussed how a Christian treats others. Look in Colossians 3:12-15, 1 Peter 3:8-10, and 1 Corinthians 13:4-8 for some insight. What are the elements of real "love" for one another? _____
_____
_____

2. Take one of those elements you've listed and pray that God will stitch it into your life in your relationships. Pray, ask others for feedback, and decide to go for it!

WEEK EIGHT

Practice Makes Perfect

THE OTHER BAND MEMBERS WERE
STARTING TO SUSPECT THAT RON HADN'T
BEEN PRACTICING AS MUCH AS HE
SHOULD HAVE BEEN.

MONDAY

A Step in God's Direction

The following are excerpts from Tom Cumber's journal.

Thursday, September 20

I've decided to keep a journal. I'm not sure why, except I want to understand a little better what knowing God is all about. I guess I hear it constantly in church. Read your Bible. Pray. Witness. Go to church. Something's not working. I'm frustrated.

I'd like to go to church at Grace, but Mom wants me to go with her. Kind of boring. But what can I say? She's been dating some guy there. I wonder what Dad would say. Not much. I haven't heard from him in six months. All those promises. Yeah, give me a break.

I can't believe I've been a Christian for four years. It sure doesn't seem like it. That summer at camp a lot of us took the plunge—John Piper, my best friend, Danny Sedgewick, Lewie Papastrano. Maybe I just wanted to get in good with some of the girls. I know Lonnie must have told me a hundred times how much she wanted me to "come to Jesus." So I did.

Or did I? And why am I writing this? I can see it now: "Bestseller: *Tom Cumber's Diary*. Unabridged." Ha.

But sometimes I wonder. Do I really know God? Is he really out there? How do I know it's true? If it is, why did Dad split?

This gets to be such a pain in the butt. (This is *my* journal. I can say anything I want—right?) If God's really there, I don't think he'll make me an ash in a flash because

185

I'm being honest. Still, if only God would do something. Prove himself. Show me for sure. I feel like that guy in the Bible who said, "I believe; help Thou mine unbelief."

Is God real? How can I know? Does anyone really know?

Oh, well. Got to get to bed. A couple prayer requests, though. I guess it can't hurt.

1. Give me and Lonnie a good time next weekend. I guess we'll just hit a movie or something.

2. Help Mom about Dad. Can't be more specific right now.

3. Help me to know you're there. Or at least to be convinced.

I'll be watching, God.

Perfect Harmony

God made us so we could know him; that's why we exist. Jesus once said, "This is eternal life: that they may know you, the only true God, and Jesus Christ, whom you have sent" (John 17:3). Paul said it even stronger: "I consider everything a loss compared to the surpassing greatness of knowing Christ Jesus my Lord" (Philippians 3:8).

Just the same, knowing God isn't quite like knowing the guy next to you at the lunch table, or your mom or dad, or even a best friend. Sometimes it feels as if God plays a universe-sized game of hide-and-seek. It seems he's out there somewhere hooting, "Bet you can't find me." And many of us yell back, "If that's the way you're going to be, I'm not playing the game."

But God may not be as far out there as we think. Paul told the Athenians that God put us where we are in time and space for a reason. Why? "So that men would seek him and perhaps reach out for him and find him, though he is not far from each one of us"(Acts 17:27).

Not far from any of us! If that's true, then where is he?

Good question. Since God is unlike us and anything we've ever known, we need to realize that if we want to see him, we might have to change our approach. What I mean is this: we see God with our heart, not with our eyes. Faith is what helps us do that.

That's too theological, you might say. Ethereal. Impractical. Weird.

Maybe so. But that's the starting point. We have faith in order that we might see. Those who want to see before believing may never believe.

Fine Tunin'

1. Ask some friends at school who are probably not Christians who and what they think God is and what he is like. Compare what they say to your own beliefs. Then ask yourself precisely why you believe differently. On what basis do you believe God exists? _____

_____

_____

2. Ask God to help you grow in faith. If Jesus were here with you now, what do you think he might tell you to do in order to learn more of him personally? _____

_____

_____

TUESDAY

Good Night, God

Wednesday, September 26

Naturally, I promptly forgot about this diary for nearly a week. No major answers to prayer yet, though Mom seems pretty decent lately.

Lonnie and I are going to see a movie Friday night. Don't know what. Probably not "R", even though I don't understand all the problems Christians have with R-rated movies.

Lonnie looked great today in class. She asked me to pray for her sister—she has a lump in her breast. I couldn't believe Lonnie asked me to do that. But she didn't turn red or anything. I like her matter-of-factness. While I opened my locker, I prayed for her sister. But what's going to happen? If the lump goes away am I to say God answered my prayer? And what if it doesn't?

Talked to John today. He's moving up to first string cornerback on the FB team. Good luck with that one.

I'm tired. Good night, God.

Did you hear that?

Funny, it makes me feel good. Just to say good night. Makes it feel a little more personal. But what if suddenly this rolling thunderous voice called down from the ceiling, "Good night, Tom"?

Yo!

Saturday, September 29

Lonnie and I had a decent time. I tried to kiss her. She let me kiss her on the cheek. Embarrassment personified!

188

She said she wasn't ready. Got to get this sex drive under control, I guess. Course I could always go to the guidance office and get my "complimentary condom." That's what Dewey calls it. Cracks me up. Some of these adults really are weird. They're so afraid we're going to catch AIDS or something. What they really ought to be doing is teaching us some morals. It makes me sick. I don't want to blow my life off because of hot hormones. But it makes me mad. Complimentary condom. Sometimes adults are stupider than us.

Lonnie told me her older sister's having more testing for breast cancer. She's married. Twenty-five or twenty-six or something. Lonnie's pretty upset. I'm going to pray about this one.

Got a C on Lorimer's French test. Mr. Henry gave us this long lecture on evolution. I actually had the guts to ask him what he thought of creation. Just to see what he would say. He answered, "We're not to discuss anything but real science in this class."

Gutless wonder, if you ask me. What are they so afraid of? Like you have to go around on tippy-toes because someone might mention the Bible. It's the one thing that makes me think it all could be true, the way so many people hate it or are afraid of it. That says something to me.

This is really interesting stuff, isn't it? It would definitely make the bestseller list, right?

Perfect Harmony

What convinces you that God is real and very much a part of this world? Miracles? Answers to prayer? People's testimonies? The Bible? Some "inner" feeling?

The Bible speaks of several ways that we know of

God and about him. One is through creation. Paul said that, "Since the creation of the world God's invisible qualities—his eternal power and divine nature—have been clearly seen, being understood from what has been made" (Romans 1:20).

In reality, though you can't know God personally simply by studying creation, you still can learn a great deal about him through it. Take the beauty of the sky as great powder puffs of clouds drift across it. Remember the last sunrise you saw? (Come on, Mark, I don't get up that early!) What about that trout you caught last summer? Or that doe and fawn you saw in the woods? What do those things tell you about God's nature? Do you think he enjoys creating beautiful things? If so, what does that show about his personality?

Roger von Oech writes in his book, *A Kick in the Seat of the Pants*: "Take a look around where you're sitting and find five things that have blue in them. Go ahead and do it.

"With a 'blue' mind-set, you'll find that blue jumps out at you; a blue book on the table, a blue pillow on the couch, blue in the painting on the wall, and so on. In like fashion, you've probably noticed that after you buy a new car, you promptly see that make of car everywhere. That's because people find what they're looking for."

Okay, so you haven't bought a new car lately. Let me talk to your dad. Maybe I can help.

But seriously, isn't that true? If you start looking for something specific like blue or loose strings or people with Macintosh computers, isn't it amazing how soon you find them? In the same way, when you begin looking for signs of God's handiwork in your life and in others—you may just see him. And sooner than you think.

Fine Tunin'

1. Take five elements of creation—from the animal and vegetable kingdoms, an insect, a color, and a kind of weather. What do each of these things demonstrate about God? Write down several thoughts. _____

_____

_____

2. Read Acts 14:15-17. What does this passage teach about how God shows us something of himself? _____

_____

_____

WEDNESDAY

When Will You Get Serious with Me, God?

Monday, October 8

Read about this guy in the news who shot some woman in the city by accident. Mother of four kids. Dead now. Gone because some druggie aimed wrong. That kind of stuff seems to happen every day now. Why does God let people like that exist? I kind of pray that God would zap them, but I don't feel right about that. I don't think God's going to convert him. So what should I pray?

For wisdom, I guess. What if they don't want it?

I talked to a new guy in the school—Travis Lurman. Basketball player, he says. Moved from Massachusetts. A bit of an accent. I always feel like I have to say something about God to people like that. But I didn't. I didn't want to offend him, I guess. But I also felt afraid. That's another thing that gets me. If God really is there, why am I afraid to talk about him?

If someone ever reads this, they'll think I landed from the planet Looped. Like Calvin in *Calvin and Hobbes*. Great comic. I can't miss that one.

Anyway, back to God. I'm not seeing anything too spectacular, God. So maybe you'd better get with the program.

The pastor said something that hit me last Sunday. (Yes, Mom, if you ever do read this, I did listen, contrary to popular belief). He talked about routine faithfulness. I got the idea he meant hanging in there, doing good, following God, doing right in the routine of life. I guess when it comes down to it, most of life is kind of a routine.

Have to think about that one, though it is a bit depressing.

Monday, October 15

Lonnie came up to me in the hallway in tears today. She said her sister definitely has cancer. I didn't know what to say. They're going to do chemotherapy. I wanted to cry with her. I tried to hug her, but her books were in the way. She begged me to pray every day.

What do you do with that kind of thing?

Had a flat today in Mom's car. Real pain. But I changed it pretty quick. My question is, how do I view those things? The pastor says God is sovereign over everything. It all happens in his plan. So was my flat his plan? Why? What's the point, besides a little irritation? Or is that just the way life is—a flat now and then?

Tuesday, October 16

I prayed three times for Lonnie's sister today. Every time I remembered. Lonnie told me she was sorry she'd cried—she'd just called home yesterday to get the results and it really upset her. And I'm worried because God doesn't seem real enough! What kind of baloney is that?

Found a passage I like—Colossians 1:9-12. Paul's prayer for the Colossians. Kind of long. But I've decided to memorize it. It'll really impress Lonnie, not that that's all I'm concerned about. (Come on, Cumber, all you care about is impressing her—be honest!) But I figure if that's what Paul prayed for people, it's the same thing I ought to pray for my family, and me, and Lonnie's family. Will see what happens.

Perfect Harmony

There are three major ways we get to know God. First, by what he has revealed about himself in the Bible—that's *cognitive* or factual knowledge. Christians believe that knowledge is infallible and without error. Second, by what others tell us they've learned about him (such as our pastor or a teacher or a friend). That's *testimonial* knowledge; it's not infallible, but it's helpful. We have to be alert, though, to any differences from what is said to what is found in the Bible. Third, we learn about God through the inner witness of the Holy Spirit, prayer, and experience. That's *personal* knowledge and it's subjective, but it's also intimate and strikes at the core of our being.

Tom realizes his need to spend time in prayer and see answers to prayer. Sometimes it helps when we keep records of the prayers we've seen answered. It can be a powerful encouragement when we go through times of darkness. As we look back on the things God did, we gain confidence that he will do more in the days up ahead.

Jesus told us, "Ask and it will be given to you; seek and you will find; knock and the door will be opened to you" (Matthew 7:7). That verse shows us one element of prayer—making requests. Prayer is much more than that—talking with God, listening, thinking, praising, expressing anger or joy, remorse or thanks.

Yet, when we do ask for something specific, like Tom did, we need to remember God may want us to do something, too. After asking we need to get up and go, to seek what we're asking. If we want a job, we will have to visit a few job sites and fill out some applications. God won't have the Burger King manager call us out of the blue. Yet, sometimes we must go farther: after filling out the application, we need to follow up with a phone call and see if we can speak with someone about getting the job. We need to knock on that door.

It's through asking, seeking, and knocking that we get to see God work. And as we see him work, we begin to realize he's there—with us, around us, before and behind us, everywhere we go.

Fine Tunin'

1. Look up two other verses on prayer and how it helps in knowing God: 1 John 5:14-15 and Colossians 1:9-12. What do these texts tell you about what to pray for and how God answers? _____

_____

_____

2. Think about keeping a diary for a month listing your prayer requests, both for yourself and others. When you see an answer, record it. Write down some thoughts about how seeing answers helped your faith in Christ. ___

_____

_____

THURSDAY

God Does Something!

Tuesday, October 23

Incredible happening. I drove into our parking lot in Mom's car. (She let me have it this afternoon to give Lonnie a ride home). I stopped at the mailbox out by the road where they keep them for the whole townhouse complex. I get out, open up the box. Suddenly, I hear this screaming. I look up and there's a car backing down and a man is caught underneath it, yelling his guts out. (I guess I would be, too).

It was like my brain suddenly went into overdrive. The car stopped because of the pressure of the man underneath it. I ran around, ripped open the door, and jammed on the brake, then put it in park. By this time, his wife was out there screeching—I couldn't understand her, they're from India. But the man underneath—I didn't know his name, they're new neighbors, but later I learned it was Aseer—was yelling that he couldn't breathe and to get the car off him. It was like my mind was clear as rainwater. I jumped back into his car, thinking I could drive it off him. But when I put the car in forward, I knew it couldn't be done without tearing off Aseer's rib cage.

I put it back in park. Then I remembered my flat. I ran to our car, opened the trunk. The jack was still lying there with the crank. (I hadn't put it back in its slot). It's a simple jack and fast. In a few seconds I had it under the car and had Aseer out. His whole back was torn to pieces, but he was okay.

I keep thinking about it. Why did I stop at the

mailbox then? I usually don't. How did it happen that the jack was so accessible, except for my flat a couple weeks ago? How was it that I was able to think so clearly and not lose my head?

I felt like a hero, and Aseer was real happy. But it all amazed me.

Was that God?

I wish I could say yes. And yet, I feel as though it has to be. How many coincidences can you have?

Lonnie also told me her sister's been getting sick from the chemo. I'm still praying. Lonnie and I are going out to a party this weekend. I'm going to kiss her. On the lips. At least I'll try. (Is that something I should pray about? Seems kind of unholy to me. But then again, if God wants to know about everything . . .)

Perfect Harmony

Every now and then, God does something incredible in our lives. Yet, often it looks like coincidence. How do we know God was in it if everything that happens can be explained by circumstances?

William Jennings Bryan, a famous Democrat, three times candidate for president of the United States, and the lawyer for the defense at the Scopes "Monkey Trial" during the early 1900s, was also an exuberant and committed Christian. He often spoke about the mystery of God. He said on one occasion, "I have observed the power of the watermelon seed. It has the power of drawing from the ground and through itself 200,000 times its weight. You tell me how it takes this material and out of it colors an outside surface beyond the imitation of art, and then forms inside of it a white rind and within that again a red heart, thickly inlaid with black seeds, each one of which in turn is capable of drawing through itself 200,000 times its weight—when you can explain to me the mystery of a watermelon, you can ask me to explain the mystery of God."[1]

God is in many ways the great mystery. Yet, think of how many things in life are a mystery—from the watermelon seed to the chickadee laying eggs to how the Monarch butterfly springs out of its cocoon. The fact that we can know God is life's greatest mystery. How can we who are small and insignificant personally be loved and known by the Infinitely Significant? How can we who are sinful and irresponsible be wholly accepted by him who is holy and all-responsible?

Answer that, and I will tell you how Tom might know it was God who arranged all those aspects of his heroism in the story above!

 Fine Tunin'

1. Read Psalm 23, the one about God as our shepherd. Why do you think this is such a valued and valuable portrait of our God? _____
_____
_____

2. Do you think God arranges the events of your life for a purpose? Read Romans 8:28, Ephesians 2:10, and Ephesians 1:11-12 and give an answer. _____
_____
_____

FRIDAY

In Love

Sunday, October 28

I kissed her!

What else can I say? It was great. I'm going to marry her. Whoa! Slow down, Cumber.

Anyway, it was great. But I won't go into any details, just in case someone reads this without my permission, *Mom!*

Monday, October 29

Still working on Colossians 1:9-12. I pray through it every day for me and Lonnie, my parents, sister, brother, and others. It does help me not to fall asleep.

I'm tired, though. I drove Lonnie home from youth group on Sunday night. Then when I dropped her off at her house, she kissed me voluntarily. Whoa! Then she asked me if I thought we were doing anything wrong. I said no. She said she was praying about it.

So I guess that makes two of us.

Oh, well. I'm in love. I feel like there's air in my body pushing me through the roof.

Wednesday, October 31

Halloween. Lonnie and I went to a youth party as Rhett Butler and Scarlett O'Hara. I dyed my hair black. Painted a little mustache on. We took a lot of pictures. Lonnie was great. This green, flouncy dress and this huge hat. It made me laugh. She held my hand. Am I a romantic or what?

We're going to visit her sister on Saturday.

Friday

I told her about my experience with Aseer. She said it had to be the "providence" of God. I looked the word up; it means God's "divine power for guiding human destiny." Not a bad idea. So what if I don't have all these incredible feelings about God. Maybe when he's there with you it doesn't matter what you feel, so long as you try to honor him.

Perfect Harmony

Feelings. They can be so good. And so bad. Sometimes.

Yet, feelings are the warm fuzzies (or cold jitters) of life. Without them, life itself would be rather boring.

How does God feel about feelings? Well, first of all, he invented them. So he must feel pretty good about them!

For another thing, God obviously wants us to experience the gamut of feelings throughout life. That's why Solomon said in Ecclesiastes, there is "a time to weep and a time to laugh, a time to mourn and a time to dance . . . a time to embrace and a time to refrain . . . a time to love and a time to hate . . ." (Ecclesiastes 3:4, 5, 8). Solomon makes it clear that such feelings are a normal and natural part of the world God has made. There is nothing wrong with good or bad feelings. It's what we do with them that counts.

At the same time, God wants us to feel something in our relationship with him. He told us to "love him with all our heart, soul, mind, and strength," right? (*See* Mark 12:30.) Doesn't that involve feelings? And what about the fruit of the Spirit—love, joy, peace. Aren't those feelings on some level?

Some Christians use an illustration of a train called *facts* pulling a coal car called *faith* with a caboose called *feelings*. The idea is when we put our faith in the facts

200

about God, we eventually get our feelings in line.

It's a good illustration. As we learn the facts about Jesus, as we obey him and put our trust in his goodness and leadership, we begin to find out what real joy, peace, and love are. It doesn't come all at once. But if it never comes, something is wrong. No Christian can go through life on raw faith without ever having some positive feelings about God, Jesus, his people, church, and the truth.

So get the facts down. Believe them. Your feelings will follow.

Fine Tunin'

1. Read some of David's feelings in Psalm 3. What does he feel as he looks around him? How does he exercise faith in the midst of his feelings? What facts does he bring to bear on them? How do the facts eventually change his feelings as he speaks of them in the last few verses? _____

_____

_____

2. Are you struggling with your feelings about the Bible, Jesus, church, and so on? If so, write down some of your feelings about one area of life—sports, friends, your job, whatever is most on your mind now. How can you relate those feelings to the kind you wish to have in your walk with Christ? _____

_____

_____

_____

WEEKEND

God Answers

Tuesday, November 6

I asked Lonnie to go steady. She said yes. I almost went through the roof.

Aseer sent me a note today, saying I'd saved his life. He asked me to come over so he can take a picture of me and my mom. We're going over tomorrow night after dinner.

Wednesday, November 7

Aseer had some Indian dessert for us, took pictures, and showed us his back. His family was very grateful. I started to tell him about what I wrote in my diary—God's providence and all. He listened and said he'd never heard an American talk like that. He knew we were mostly Christians, but he said he rarely met any Americans who spoke about it. Anyway, he said he'd like to talk again sometime.

The other day I was standing at my locker and Lonnie came by and wriggled in between me and the locker and whispered— *real* sweetly—"How you doin', handsome?" Flashing her deep brown eyes. I almost sank into the floor.

We saw her sister last weekend. She didn't look too bad. We didn't talk about the cancer, just said we were praying for her. Lonnie kept telling me not to bring up anything except that we were praying. I got the impression her sister's pretty sensitive about it.

I keep thinking about my relationship with God. I am praying more, and memorizing Scripture. I guess it feels better, more real. But I wonder if this is what it's like for most of us. "Routine faithfulness," like Pastor Degan said. Just hanging in there and doing right in the routine of life, even when it's not exciting or interesting.

Anyway, I feel as though God is speaking to me. Through Aseer. Through Lonnie. In my heart. I don't know where it's going. But I'm going to keep this diary, keep writing down what happens. It's nice to see what I thought earlier in the year. Already I feel as though I've come a long way. I guess I'm a little excited, in a way. I feel as though life is an adventure. And if you believe God's orchestrating it, then it gets even better.

I don't know. Probably tomorrow I'll be as doubtful as ever. But one thing I do know: LONNIE—I LOVE YOU!

Perfect Harmony

One of the best ways to discover how we feel about God is to look at how we feel about his people. Christians not only love God, we also love one another. In fact, John said that our love for God is directly comparable to how we love others. If we don't love his people, we certainly don't love him (*see* 1 John 4:20-21).

Furthermore, we often learn best about God by what we see in his people—as recorded in the Bible and as pictured by those we live with and go to church with. There is power in a good example.

Tom was beginning to look for God in many ways in his life—through the events that occurred, through answers to prayer, through his relationship with his girlfriend and others, through the Bible. Relating to God in Christ is like a lifelong friendship. There's talk and silence.

There're times when he's close, times when he seems far away. There're times when you're high on each other, and times when you're angry. All of it, though, is God's way of giving us the fullness of his love and blessing.

Of course, there's also a caution in all this: we can't put God in a box. We often develop expectations of him that don't come to pass. We end up disappointed and even disillusioned.

But again, that's all part of learning to relate to him. Like C. S. Lewis wrote of Aslan, the lion symbol of Christ in *The Chronicles of Narnia*, "He's . . . not like a tame lion." A relationship with anyone including God has surprises, triumphs, setbacks, twists, turns, false starts, temporary ends, and new beginnings. It's all part of your story—and his story in your life.

Seek him and you will find him more than you ever imagined. But also different that you ever expected!

Fine Tunin'

1. Look at what Paul says about example in Philippians 3:17. Name three people you know who exemplify good Christian character. What traits do they display that you most admire? _____

_____

_____

2. Take one of the traits mentioned above and begin praying that God will make it real in your life.

Note

1. William Jennings Bryan, cited in *Reader's Digest*, August 1983, 133.

PERFECT HARMONY

Relationships are what life is all about. They're what make the living worth living. When I look back on some of my friendships, I realize that when God saw it wasn't good for Adam to be alone, he saw it straight. We need people. We need good vibrations. We need words and encouragement and friendship. We need one another.

Music is one of the true joys and elixirs of life. Personally, I like to listen to all types of performers and groups, both classical and rock, sacred and secular. As you've read this book, I hope you've begun to see that relationships are like a good piece of music. They touch the emotions, they thrill us, they mellow us out, they rise and fall, climax and peter out. To make beautiful music, though, takes practice, effort, a ready knowledge of the basics, and a commitment to the principles. When one has all those elements in line, most of us can at least carry a tune. We can sing together and make it sound good.

Do you ever feel as though you do nothing but blow it in your relationships? Maybe you've treated them too lightly, as if everything should naturally work out. It doesn't. You have to work at it to make it work out.

Still, when a relationship does work, it carries with it a beauty—a harmony and melody—that can make every moment an adventure and a thrill. Rarely have I been disappointed when I've worked to cultivate a friendship. People respond hungrily and happily to those who care for them sincerely.

Rockin' or reelin', knockin' or kneelin', I hope you

will approach your relationships like you would in performing a worthy piece of music. As you play, get caught up in it. Smile. Let the melody carry you.

And as the notes wing higher, open your eyes. Those who are listening will be smiling, too.

So tune up, tune in, and never tune out your Lord, your loved ones, your friends, or your church members. Together we all make music that God says he expects to enjoy forever.

HAVE YOU HERD THE NEWS?

Beefin' Up, the wildly popular teen devotional by the author of *Tunin' Up*, is also available from Multnomah Press!

- Do you ever feel like a Bar T brand in a Bar S world?
- Are you able to stand your ground when the rest of the herd is stampeding away from God?
- Do you stand around chewing your cud, or are you moo-ving ahead?

Becoming a strong Christian doesn't just happen. If you want to grow, you've got to feed on the truths of God's word. This eight week devotional will give you the milk and meat you need to beef up your faith. Udderly.

So break out of the herd! *Beefin' Up* is *Daily Feed for Amazing Grazing*. Hoof it on down to your local Christian bookstore for your copy of *Beefin' Up*!